D1268333

TEACHING
AND PERFORMING:

IDEAS FOR ENERGIZING
YOUR CLASSES

TEACHING AND PERFORMING:

IDEAS FOR ENERGIZING YOUR CLASSES

William M. Timpson
Colorado State University

Suzanne Burgoyne
University of Missouri-Columbia

Christine S. Jones
Colorado State University

Waldo Jones
University of Northern Colorado

Magna Publications
Madison, Wisconsin

© 1997 Magna Publications, Inc.
2718 Dryden Drive
Madison, WI 53704
Printed in the United States of America
03 01 00 99 98 97   8 7 6 5 4 3 2 1

Cover design by Evan Schultz

Library of Congress Cataloging-in-Publication Data

Teaching and performing: ideas for energizing your classes/ William M.
    Timpson ... [et al.].
        p.cm
    Includes bibliographical references (p.) and index.
    ISBN 0-912150-44-0
    1. College teaching. 2. Performing arts. I. Timpson, William M.
LB2331.T34 1997
378.1'25--dc20   96-46235
                                                            CIP

Dedication

to Nick Burlak — actor, director, producer, and performer in the most dramatic of roles on the world's stage of history. May your courage, energy and charisma inspire others.

Table of Contents

Acknowledgments

There are so many people and organizations to thank for support and assistance on this project. To start, we need to recognize all the groundbreaking work that went into the 1982 publication of *Teaching as Performing*, which Bill Timpson co-authored with David Tobin. Here we must repeat our appreciation for all the ideas we received from teachers at all levels who joined us in workshops and courses. Fortunately, we were able to capture many of these performance lessons in print and on videotape for later use. Throughout this period, Barbara Nelson, education professor at Colorado State University, supported our explorations and helped us frame this material within a larger context of effective communications and instruction.

Once this work pushed into a more focused look at teaching and performance in higher education, Bill received invaluable help and ideas from colleagues at Colorado State University, the University of California-Santa Cruz, and the University of Queensland in Brisbane, Australia. When Suzanne Burgoyne, Christine Jones, and Waldo Jones joined this project, they drew on their own circles of colleagues at campuses where they have held positions — Suzanne at Creighton University and the University of Missouri-Columbia, Christine at Colorado State, and Waldo at the University of Northern Colorado.

Equally important as the teachers in our lives are people from all walks of life who have worked with each of us on staged productions over the years, people who have given so much of themselves — their time, energy, and talents — to bring works to life. In particular, we want to acknowledge the staff, cast, and crew from Openstage Theatre, the Larimer Chorale, and the Canyon Concert Ballet, as well as theatre productions at Creighton University and the University of Missouri-Columbia. Special thanks here to Gailmarie Kimmel for recruiting Bill back into the special magic of performances that built on widespread community support.

We also want to acknowledge the contributions of the staff and television crew at the Office of Instructional Services at Colorado State University — in particular, Mike Ellis, Larry Preuss, Bill Kruse, Fred Rosenkranz, and Pres Davis — for helping us preserve so many superb performances on videotape. These tapes have been broadcast nationally and are available for purchase through Magna Publications, Inc.

As this manuscript moved toward completion, we also received valuable feedback from a variety of readers. We applaud each one of them. For her contributions on film references, Gloria Campbell deserves special recognition.

Finally, we extend our heartfelt appreciation to our editors at Magna Publications — Robert Magnan, Linda Babler, and Richard Perkins — for their support and patience as this manuscript evolved through various stages and revisions. Bob took the lead in providing both general support for this project as well as detailed critiques along the way and we are deeply indebted to him, for his tireless attention to both the big questions and all those subtle details that can make or break a published work.

Foreword
from the Classroom

by Bill Timpson

In the late 1970s I was actively developing a variety of workshops for teachers at all levels. Fresh ideas and titles could attract new students. Some who enrolled were colleagues from my own campus at Colorado State University. One offering that quickly proved both popular and practical addressed the parallels between teaching and the stage. Having performed in a community dance troupe, local ballet productions, various choirs, musicals, and operas, I knew firsthand the benefits for my own teaching. Whenever we discussed teaching as art and science, I could always draw on my experiences on stage to support and energize classroom practice.

What became an experimental offering on campus evolved first into an article and then a book for Prentice-Hall. Written with my colleague, Dave Tobin, and published in 1982, *Teaching as Performing* introduced teachers at all levels to relevant skills and practices from the stage.

The first experimental workshop offerings then became a regular component of an annual graduate course on communications and presentation skills. Over a four-week period, teachers would plan, script, and stage one particular idea. With a performer's approach to voice and movement, costuming, sets, lighting and props, characterization, and direction, these teachers would rehearse their pieces in front of guest "directors" called in to offer feedback. On the last day of class, these teachers would then perform in front of classmates, friends, and, at times, television cameras brought in to ensure a visual record.

Over the years, I have found the results from this line of work to be quite dramatic, as teachers at all levels have pushed themselves to learn more about performance, develop new skills and attitudes, and create something provocative and practical for their students. Along the way, these teachers also pushed me and my collaborators, deepening our own understanding of the performing processes that underlie dynamic and engaging instruction.

In many ways, then, these performances have served as benchmarks, models of exemplary teaching that were rehearsed and refined over time. The excitement generated with each performance has also served as a model for renewal, giving these teachers a way to rekindle their own excitement by finding fresh and creative ways to approach familiar material.

My colleagues and I now offer you this extension of that first book, with another decade of exploration and development added, here with a more specific focus on teaching in higher education. Suzanne Burgoyne brings a lifetime of work in academia and the theatre, including acting and directing at the university level, maintaining active research interests (in translating a Belgian playwright, in particular), as well as leading workshops on performance skills for colleagues at Creighton and Missouri. Christine Jones brings years of experience as a director and actor, as a teacher at the university level and in the schools with expertise in teacher education and staff development, and as a collaborator with me in a graduate class on performance skills for teachers. Waldo Jones also brings years of experience as an actor and director, as a teacher in higher education and secondary schools, and as a consultant for theatrical applications in personnel practices for businesses, industries, and agencies.

Important to the spirit and integrity of this book is that we four remain active as teachers, performers, and researchers. Individually, we continue to play various roles in the performing arts — singing, dancing, acting, directing, consulting, assisting, taking advanced classes, and so on. Individually, we continue to explore applications of performance skills to our own teaching and conduct workshops for other teachers.

Case Studies

In what follows I summarize interviews with two colleagues who bring a lot of the performer's zest to their teaching. I think you will find their comments intriguing and useful as a lead-in to this book.

Dr. Janice Moore

Dr. Janice Moore is a professor of biology with an enviable publication record, an ambitious new book underway, the job of director of the Biocore Program at Colorado State University, and a real gift for teaching. Routinely, she takes on the department's large introductory classes. She is successful with them, in part because of her extensive performance background.

I've known Janice for several years and watched her lecture. Her expertise, skill, energy, and joy in teaching are quickly evident. Even the smallest of mollusks looms larger when she lectures — its evolution miraculous, its mysteries basic to understanding our universe. Knowing that she had an extensive background as a performer intrigued me; I wanted to explore her insights into the teaching/performing connection.

From an early age, Janice regularly sang solos in church services. In high school she received awards for public speaking. At Rice University she parlayed her singing talents into working with a rock 'n' roll band, performing every day one summer and intermittently thereafter. In college she acted in some melodramas and wrote and directed several one-act plays for an intramural competition, earning first- and second-place awards.

As we talked, she offered a number of observations and insights about the connection between teaching and the stage.

WMT: What did you bring over to teaching from performance?

JM: All of it! I can usually get students' attention and keep it. Students can see me as enthusiastic, interesting. On the negative side, they do say they want more AV stuff, but I know that I always saw slides and films as distracting when I was a student. They also want me to hand out lecture notes, but I believe that students think more if they have to pay attention.

WMT: What do you do with stage awareness?

JM: With a lower-division class of 200, for example, I don't need to update the facts in my notes at the same rate as I have to for upper-division classes, so I can think about teaching more. At the beginning, I'll joke, talk about the weekend, show some empathy, get their attention. If I see students are drifting off, I'll stop and ask what's going on. I'll try something different. On stage one can't depart from your script or song, but I can change my physical relationship with the audience. In class I can do the same. I'll move out towards my students. Out front there are fewer obstructions. I can project more energy.

WMT: How has performing prepared you for teaching?

There is no better preparation for teaching than performing, because the challenges are the same — getting people's attention and holding it. (*Note:* Joseph Lowman concluded in *Mastering the Techniques of Teaching* that the two most important qualities for college teachers to achieve in class are intellectual excitement and rapport with students. *WMT*)

WMT: What about energy?

JM: As a teacher, I try to remember how it feels to be a student. I know that I felt timid. I imagine myself as a student for about five minutes or so before class. In this way I remind myself what it's like to be in my own class, to whom it is that I'm talking.

It's important for a performer to get in tune with an audience, for a teacher to be in tune with students, but it's more difficult to relate to students. As a teacher, you have to welcome all student questions; there are more individual interactions. That's different for a performer.

In a performance, the audience will pull for you. They want a good show. They're your friends. In that sense performance is more satisfying. Unfortunately, not all students want to be there. Students often assume an antagonistic relationship with their teachers. Histories and values clash.

WMT: Costuming?

JM: Absolutely the same importance for performing and teaching. For example, I always wear a dress when I teach. It's always "Dr. Moore" with undergrads. I'm not just another student. It's part of the act. Students may like teachers who dress and act like them, but I think the subtle barrier is important. In my classes, my authority equals my expertise and contributes to their motivation to learn.

Primates learn better from superiors, not subordinates or equals. Admittedly, there may be gender differences here. Women professors have less perceived authority. Consequently, they must dress the part more.

I also believe that it is disrespectful of audiences for a performer or a teacher to dress carelessly. Even grunge bands put thought into their image. Male teachers should wear a sport coat and tie or a vest — something "non-student."

WMT: What about preparation time?

JM: Here, there is a big difference. You cannot perfect a lesson as you might a stage performance. You give it once a year. It's more like writing for a newspaper with its daily deadlines than trying to perfect a novel.

WMT: Props?

JM: I do need to use more. As a student, however, I didn't like to sit in the dark and try to take notes. That's why I don't like slides. I use overheads, but in a lit room. Yet I know that some students miss parts of the lecture and could use something up on a screen. If the overheads are detailed, however, students are just copying; they're not thinking. I could just as easily provide a handout.

Sometimes I do provide little toys as prizes — gimmicks for winning a quiz, for example. I'll give out a wind-up crab or something else funny and weird.

I suppose I could do more to make things more interesting with multi-media. Again, one runs into the newspaper deadline problem. I have produced multi-media shows for conference presentations, for example, but that can require all-consuming prep time. Much of the commercially available AV material is aimed well below college-level students.

WMT: In the theatre, we talk about "raising the stakes," making it important for an audience to care. What do you do in class?

JM: I'll use the building block concept. For example, "Pay attention to this. You'll see it again." Or "This will be on the exam" — although I rarely use this one.

WMT: What do you do for a hook, that theatrical device used to engage the audience early on in a production?

JM: I may say something like, "This is important or neat because ..." or this one trait — whatever — is the basis for much of what we'll study in the next two weeks. I try to give unmistakable emphasis to things that deserve it.

WMT: Any use of warm-up before teaching?

JM: On my good days — when I'm energetic, upbeat, feeling good — I may tease students or joke with them. I'll pay attention to them, talk to some. On bad days — when I'm down or tired — I'll just start the lecture.

Teaching takes a different kind of energy. As a performer, you can fake it. You can certainly fake some things as a teacher, but it's hard to do the personal interaction part of teaching when you're cranky. On bad days you can just do your job and teach, whereas as a performer you get more positive feedback. An audience can pull you up and out. Students don't do that as much. They're like a nameless crowd. Many of them do not want a teacher to know who they are! There is a danger in that some teacher "performers" can get sucked or hooked into pleasing students and this then becomes a goal. For me, the goal always has to be teaching; the performance is simply a way to do it.

WMT: Any other insights into the impact of performance on your teaching?

JM: I'm in demand as a speaker. I play with my audiences. Whenever I talk about my cockroaches, audiences love it. I give very playful research seminars. My attitude is that my audiences should have a good time. I know that I'm having a good time and that's a key. It gives me energy, makes me enthusiastic. If I'm not having a good time, no one else will.

Dr. Carol Mitchell

Dr. Carol Mitchell is another friend and colleague, an associate professor in the English Department at Colorado State University. A folklorist by training, she has recently toured the Middle East and helped begin a new course on goddesses in literature. She is intriguing because, unlike Janice Moore, she has not performed, but thoroughly enjoys her teaching and brings a lot of the performance skill into class — i.e., costuming, energy, self-awareness, "stage presence" (awareness of what is happening in class with the content, the students, and the dynamics). In fact, she really is not interested in traditional performance; she prefers the spontaneity of creating something new in class over the demands of memorizing lines for the stage.

Carol is energetic and intense, but friendly and fun, alive with ideas — someone who combines a genuine love of teaching with an active intellectual interest in folklore, Asian literature, mythology, and goddess studies. As a high school English teacher, she learned how to keep the interest of her students or suffer the consequences — i.e., if students found her boring, they would quickly create their own diversions.

WMT: Do you think about your costumes?

CM: I do make great use of costuming in class. In my Asian Lit and Folklore classes, I'll wear different examples of clothing which I have collected over the years. It's not uniformly true, but some students do respond positively, mostly the females. It adds some interest. For others, mostly the males — and this tends to be a classic gender difference — what I wear is of only passing interest.

More generally, though, what I wear does affect my teaching. They are watching me. I like clothes; I like jewelry. Clothes are an art form. When I think I look good, I have more confidence and perform better.

Earlier in my career, when I was teaching high school, I felt I had to dress up more because I was so close in age to the students, and short, and I looked young. I still believe that my high heels made a difference, especially among the males. At the university, I know now that no one will confuse me with being a student, but I still wear more formal clothes, "different" slacks from what the students will wear, for example. I am in charge; my class is not a democracy.

WMT: Talk about being "center stage."

CM: I enjoy being the center of attention when teaching, so I have to be careful to give students enough chance to talk to each other. Yet they have limited knowledge and I am the expert here: I do know more.

Being center stage fuels my enthusiasm, which in turn helps me energize students about the material. But I don't teach in a vacuum; student feedback is critical. The way the class clicks makes a difference. Teaching is very dynamic; so is all performance. My Asian Lit and Goddess classes are giving a lot back to me and I tell my students how important that is for me, how much I appreciate it.

One class, my worst ever, just would not respond, no matter what I did. It was so strange because in previous years I had never had this kind of problem. I liked the material. So I finally gave up on them as a group and concentrated on teaching to those two or three who were responding. That made all the difference.

WMT: What do you do about preparation before class? With reflections after?

CM: At least a half-hour before class, I know I'm getting up for it. I know that's what I do. I'm reviewing my notes, but not just to refresh my memory. I'm also getting in the right mood. And I do get high from teaching, especially after good classes. I'm up. But it is a downer when I feel class has gone poorly.

I'm not conscious of reflecting on my teaching right after class; often students are coming up after class. I'm more likely to think about it at home, sometimes when I'm getting ready for bed. For example, recently I had this interaction with a particular student in class about religion. I was claiming that Christianity, with its linear conceptualization of time, began with creation and then moved through the cataclysmic second coming and a transformation of the earth into heaven, while other religions saw life and the earth in a more cyclical fashion with a continuous repetition of life, death, and reincarnation. Anyway, she didn't agree and it seemed to me that we were just talking past each other. It was later that night that I got this insight into why we were missing, so I started off the next class with that same issue, but it wasn't planned.

Whether I think about teaching also depends on the people around me. If I know that someone else enjoys talking about teaching, I'll often talk about it. It's fun to chat about. In fact, we have a group which gets together weekly for dinner and we often talk about our teaching.

WMT: Do you think about sets or props?

CM: I prefer to have classes with movable desks and chairs. It's really frustrating to be stuck in a classroom with everything bolted. It's hard to do any group work. I also tend to avoid using a podium; I like to use the front table of class.

If I have a small class, I'll often pass around pictures. For some classes, I now do more with slides. I can point out the details, although slides can be distracting. Some students have a hard time looking at slides and listening to me at the same time.

I know that I play with my glasses, and that's been a change. And sometimes I have a book I refer to.

WMT: Are you conscious of your movements in class?

CM: I move around, in part, to give students something to watch, but I also want to have them keep their focus on me. We are a culture that focuses on action, not being. Accordingly, staying rooted behind a podium is a problem. I am conscious of my movements. Sometimes if I notice some students who are chatting or seem inattentive, I'll walk toward them, and that will usually correct the problem. Having taught high school, I have no problem confronting discipline.

Periodically, I will note the effect of a certain gesture, but rarely is there any time during class to stop and reflect but for just the briefest of moments. There's just too much going on; I could never plan to repeat it. I guess it just gets stored somewhere in my unconscious and plays out somehow in the future.

WMT: Are you conscious of the role you play when you teach?

CM: I'm really not a different character in class. It's all one, integrated, the teacher and me, although I'm a bit more formal when I teach. However, there was this one time — this was funny — when the teacher in me took over outside of class. I was in a bar with a friend and someone I didn't know sat down next to me and soon we were in a conversation and, before I knew it, I was giving a lecture, until I stopped myself and we both laughed. You see, the teacher is me.

WMT: What do you do with humor in class? With emotions?

CM: I do enjoy myself in class and humor is part of it. I often tease my students and joke with them. I tell jokes about myself, mostly off the cuff. I like to hear laughter in my classes.

But I also can exhibit the full range of emotions. My students have also seen me angry, sad, serious. I want to respond as a whole person, and I want them to do the same, to react holistically, integrating mind and body, not divorcing their emotions. At the university, we focus too much on the intellect alone, on reason. Nothing is that simple or unconnected.

WMT: It's fun to watch you teach. You have such enthusiasm.

CM: I like teaching. It's especially fun again, now that I have had my sabbatical. I've had a great break — reading, travel. I needed that space from teaching. The public and the legislature really don't realize how draining teaching can be. School teachers need their summers off to recover, to get their emotional energy back. The U.S. just does not want to recognize the emotional needs of people.

Final Thoughts

Despite testimonials from gifted teachers like Moore and Mitchell, this mixing of performance and teaching may irritate some in higher education. Especially on those campuses where research is the pre-eminent concern, we have to acknowledge that interest in teaching may have limited career benefits. Those who receive awards for their teaching may even be suspected of being winners of "popularity contests." Accordingly, a focus on the performance skills of teachers might seem doubly dangerous, even heretical, especially for younger faculty on the tortuous tenure track.

On the contrary, we will argue. Whether you want to improve your delivery or do more to inspire students, whether you want to do more to engage students in critical and creative thinking or deepen their learning, we know you will gain much from studying the use of performance skills and practice in teaching.

In the long run, you have to face yourself in the mirror as a teacher. Can you improve? Do your students deserve better? We are convinced that performing skills can go far to help you sharpen your delivery skills, energize your teaching, and do more to motivate and challenge your students.

Foreword
from the Stage

by Suzanne Burgoyne

I met Bill Timpson through the Kellogg National Fellowship Program, a three-year fellowship for leadership training and interdisciplinary studies. The program is based on the philosophy that, as contemporary civilization demands increasingly focused specialization, it also requires leaders with a generalist perspective, leaders who have a view of the "whole picture" and can communicate across disciplinary boundaries. Each year, the Kellogg Foundation selects a class of 40-50 mid-career professionals, from a variety of fields, who attend bi-annual seminars on such topics as public policy, technology and change, etc. The individual fellows also pursue independent study projects that take each fellow outside of his or her primary field of specialization. Bill and I were Class II Fellows (1981-84).

I came to the fellowship program as a theatre professional interested in exploring how theatre techniques could be used for pedagogy in other fields. As an education professional with an interest in performance, Bill had already done work applying performance methodology to teacher training. With Bill's encouragement, I eventually developed "teaching as performance" workshops for faculty on my home campus and elsewhere. Together, Bill and I presented workshops for Kellogg Fellowship gatherings, in which we used theatre-based methods to examine the particular social issues being considered in the seminar.

My belief that theatre has contributions to make in addressing the many challenges facing our civilization led me to apply for the fellowship. One of the problems inherent in over-specialization, however, is that people outside a given field usually don't know much about what is actually going on in that field — and often hold stereotyped images of the field and its practitioners.

Theatre, in particular, falls prey to such misunderstandings. When I applied for the Kellogg Fellowship, one of the interviewers asked, "Are you sure you're not just a frustrated actress?" And, at the first meeting of Class II, a member of the advisory committee told me, "When we were planning this fellowship program, it never occurred to us that a theatre person might have something to contribute."

As Elyse Pineau (1994) points out, the prejudice against theatre also rears its ugly head whenever anyone suggests that theatre might have something to contribute to "the very serious business of education" (5). Pineau observes that "the ideology of American formal education has been constructed largely on models of technology, industry, and corporate bureaucracy" (4). Thus, analogies between teaching and the performing arts provoke disgruntled critics such as Ralph Smith (1979, 7) to claim that "if the acting analogy were carried to its logical extreme, a teacher who took it seriously would never have to understand anything."

Certainly, those of us investigating the relationship between teaching and the performing arts have never advocated that the teacher become a "mere entertainer" in the classroom. Furthermore, Smith reveals in his comment a naïveté about what a good actor actually does. In order to portray a role, an actor (like a teacher) engages in research, studying the historical period in which the play is set and all the social, political, and cultural factors that influence the character. During rehearsal, the actors and the director explore the characters' interactions with each other and with their environment — by acting them out.

By the time of the performance, actors can be convincing in their portrayal because their understanding of the play — and of why their characters act as they do — has moved from the intellectual to the experiential plane; the research has been assimilated and embodied by the actor. While an actor does acquire specific vocal and physical skills that enhance communication (training from which the teacher, too, can benefit), the technical skills are not the heart of the actor's art any more than they are of the teacher's pedagogy. The heart of the actor's art has to do with a lifelong exploration of the nature of the human condition (e.g., Miller 1967; Bates 1987) — a "very serious business," indeed.

So why does the prejudice against theatre persist? Certainly, media hype perpetuates stereotyped and negative images of performers. However, the prejudice against theatre has a long history, which Jonas Barish (1981, 2) traces in *The Antitheatrical Prejudice* and calls "a kind of ontological malaise."

Studying manifestations of the prejudice in philosophers from Plato to Nietzsche, Barish observes that the actor is often equated with the liar, someone pretending to be what she or he is not. Even more fundamental to the problem, Barish argues, is that the protean actor, capable of transforming himself or herself into someone else, raises doubts about the stability of human identity.

For philosophers such as Plato, who advocate a stable society with everyone firmly implanted in fixed social roles, theatre is dangerous because the actor's ability to change roles suggests that other people, too, could change. Plato envisioned a highly specialized society, based on a "monolithic theory of personality ... [which] reduces each man to a single well-defined entity, firmly linked to his social role" (Barish 1981, 21-23) and the ideal of an all-powerful state that would form the characters of its citizens through education. As Barish points out, for Plato, individual freedom "carries the seeds of diversity and hence of disruption" (20).

In Plato's view, mimesis (imitation, theatre) is a powerful educational tool and must be controlled by the state. Believing that people become what they imitate, Plato would prohibit students from acting roles other than those of persons of their own social and professional class, sex, and "moral outlook" (Barish 1981, 21). The educational system must suppress "anything in the intellectual diet that encourages freedom, curiosity, or exploration" (19), including "the whole realm of unstructured play, of spontaneous self-discovery, of casual and random improvisation" (22). Students must not discover the possibility that they might become anything other than what the state has predetermined they should be.

Whereas modern critics dismiss theatre as "mere entertainment," not "serious business," Plato wanted to banish the dramatic poet from his utopian Republic precisely because he viewed the theatre as a potent instrument of change and thus a threat to social stability. Furthermore,

Barish (1981, 8) observes, "the poets were being inflated into the rivals of the philosophers as the basis for intellectual training." Ironically, Plato testified to his belief in the power of drama by couching his attack on it in the form of a drama — a dialogue.

Whereas the ideal of stable societies and identities may offer an appealing image of security, that ideal has been undermined in the twentieth century by new discoveries in all fields, by the ever-accelerating change that accompanies rapid technological development, and by an intense probing into the nature of human identity. Phenomenologist Bruce Wilshire (1982, 230) argues that theatre serves as a laboratory for identity, necessary to the process of individuation for audiences as well as actors. Like Plato, Wilshire proposes that theatre can stimulate change: "Theatre is an art which reaches out to encompass and thematize possibilities of personality change within the remarkably commodious matrix of identity of self."

Futurists warn us the pace of change will continue to accelerate. Charles Swanson (1980) cites Alvin Toffler (1974) in suggesting that theatre training can help students learn to cope with the future. Borrowing the language of management, Swanson argues that educational theatre trains students to function well in ad hoc organizations, in which a group forms to perform a particular task (in the case of theatre, to put on a play) and then disbands. Furthermore, theatre students change roles and tasks from production to production. Such experiences prepare students to deal with a world in which they may need to change careers several times.

Pointing out that most educational systems imitate the manufacturing model, Swanson (1980, 63) proposes that "students are experientially programmed toward an intolerance of change by the regimented organization of schools." He cites a pilot study which indicated that, whereas "students in regular classrooms became more rigid (less able to change), ... theatre students became more open (more able to cope with change)" (64). In an era in which organizational specialists train managers to function in an environment of change, Swanson notes,

> While businessmen are condemning theatre in schools as a luxury or a frill, their consultants are using techniques based on role-playing, scenarios, and simulations (we [in theatre] call them 'improvisations'). Many of the techniques for management and organizational development are thus adapted from theatre.

I do not mean to suggest that theatre has all the answers. Debates about methodology, pedagogy, and goals abound in theatre, as in other disciplines. I do, however, mean to suggest that theatre is more than "mere entertainment" and that critiques of the contributions theatre can make to education often suffer from the distortions of the anti-theatrical prejudice and/or from lack of familiarity with current developments in the discipline.

For instance, Peter McLaren (1988, 165) posits three types of educators: the teacher-as-liminal servant, the teacher-as-entertainer, and the teacher-as-hegemonic overlord. Basing his discussion of the second type upon the separation of actors and audience and the presumed passivity of the latter, McLaren critiques the teacher-as-entertainer:

> When students were actively engaged by the instructor but ... remained isolated and unreflective viewers of the action, then the students were in the process of being entertained. The classroom was transformed into a theatre and the students constituted an audience.
>
> In this instance, the teacher assumed an entertainment role: as a propagandist — or even worse, an evangelist — for dominant cultural, economic, or ethical interests.

While theatre can indeed function as a means of reinforcing hegemonic structures — and the new historiographers among theatre historians are busily analyzing how certain theatres have served that purpose (e.g., Postlewait and McConachie 1989) — performances can also critique a dominant social order and provide alternative role models and imagined futures (e.g., Hornby 1986).

The audience/performance relationship provides a fertile field of debate and experimentation within the discipline of theatre, generating approaches that can contribute to classroom pedagogy. How "unreflective" is an audience member? Drawing upon "reader response" theory, some scholars view the spectator as an active participant in the construction of meaning (see, for instance, Cole 1992). Major twentieth-century theatrical theorist/practitioners from Brecht (1964) to Grotowski (1968) have sought means to jolt the spectator out of passivity and into active engagement. Experiments with the arrangement of the theatrical space, from arena and thrust stages to environmental theatre, have explored the impact of spatial organization on the audience. Theatre artists committed to social change, such as

Augusto Boal (1979) often seek to involve audiences actively in the creation of the performance.

In order for our educational system to remain vital, disciplines must not become the narrow, rigid, carefully separated specialties that Plato envisioned. Systems theorists point out that closed systems, which "operate in relative isolation from the environment," usually "continue to operate in the same way in spite of environmental changes" and thus "suffer entropy — death from internal chaos." Open systems, on the other hand, are "in constant contact with [their] environment" and thus are "adaptive to environmental needs" (Swanson 1980, 62).

Just as Bill and I continue to learn from each other's disciplinary perspectives, we hope you will find our suggestions about the intersections between theatre and education stimulating to your own growth as a teacher. Much of actor training, though based upon theory, is conducted through active, experiential learning methods. We have included numerous exercises in the book; we encourage you to try them. We ask you to peruse these pages with an open mind — and not to succumb to the anti-theatrical prejudice.

Chapter 1
Introduction

Good teaching in higher education requires expertise and planning. Great teachers add energy, excitement, and sensitivity. Most teachers work in isolation, developing their skills through periodic feedback from students, both formal and informal, as well as their own intuitive feel and desire to improve. A few teachers actively seek feedback and direction from peers and others. Yes, great teachers are born and, yes, great teachers are bred, but it's rather pointless to try to untangle the exact contribution of each. Every great teacher combines natural talents with skills learned along the way.

And so it is with great actors. Training, direction, and regular feedback combine with natural gifts and personal motivation to make performances memorable. Having been working with these ideas since the late 1970s, we are confident that there is much in the performing arts that can help teachers become great. In this book we will describe those lessons from the stage and how they can help you become more self-aware, sharpen your delivery, engage your students more effectively, and promote deeper learning and more critical and creative thinking by students.

Expertise and preparation are essential starting points, but an energetic delivery and the creative use of classroom time and resources can help you inspire students to think and learn more, to consider new possibilities and develop new skills. Indeed, even the best lecture notes cannot guarantee learning when teachers are uninspired or when they come to class prepared only to read those notes. Drawing from our own training and experiences, as well as those of the many teachers with whom we have worked on various campuses, we offer

you what we believe are fresh insights into your own teaching as well
as new designs for more engaging learning experiences.

Parallels
Between Classroom and Stage

Both are essentially live public performances where delivery and
engagement matter. Audiences for each may be quite large. Both
require preparation. Indeed, effectiveness in teaching can be measured by some of the same criteria as used for performers. Could the
teacher be heard? Seen? Was the material organized well? Did the
teacher's timing increase engagement? Was good use made of the
classroom space and the other resources available?

Good teaching means much more than giving information. In this
day of desktop publishing, class notes are easily updated and repro-
duced. Although departmental budgets might not permit regular dis-
tribution of such notes, they could be made available to students to
copy or on reserve at the library. Why not use class time for interactions, debates, discussions, questions, role-plays, activities, opportunities to practice new skills — all meaningful ways to use the talents
assembled in your classroom? Few people would attend performances where scripts are merely read. They want more. And so do
students. Great teachers will use many of the same skills as great
performers to bring their subjects to life.

Instruction and Entertainment

Yet there is resistance to the notion that performers have anything
to offer teachers. One frequent comment notes the distinction between instruction and entertainment. Trained and rewarded as subject area experts, many teachers are understandably sensitive when
they are judged on delivery. Few have had any formal training in
presentation skills. Some even dismiss instructor popularity as pandering to students, valuing form over substance and entertainment
over instruction.

At the top of any list on teaching effectiveness, however, should be
student learning. To be successful here, we will argue, requires much
more indeed than subject matter expertise. It requires some mastery
of delivery — especially in large classes — as well as some skill in

engaging the minds and hearts of students, in challenging them to consider new possibilities and rethink old ideas, in helping them learn better how to learn.

While some of this may seem threatening to those teachers who want to remain narrowly defined as subject matter experts only, others will embrace those lessons from the stage that can help them master some new skills. With some training, practice, and a commitment to learning from feedback, we can say with confidence that you will learn quickly. After all, as a student and now a teacher, you already have a wealth of classroom experience.

Performance Anxiety and Fun

One understandable fear involves public speaking, an unavoidable challenge for teachers. Many people are anxious about being up in front of a group, especially a large one; some are terrified. And so it is true for countless actors and other performers. The key is to learn how to channel those feelings in a constructive direction, a process that can turn debilitating anxiety into useful motivation for improvement. Performers must confront their anxiety over the years; what they learn in so doing can help teachers.

The flip side to this, of course, is the joy that can come from succeeding in front of others — audiences or students. Working through complex material, probing understanding, connecting different viewpoints, citing relevant sources, telling stories of discovery and dead ends, noting the shifting paradigms, correcting misconceptions, answering questions, reminding people of old truths, or inspiring others with new insights — the energy exchange here can be quite thrilling.

The Making of Teachers and Actors

Because teachers are "born" and "made," every teacher has the potential to be great. Some may come blessed with more "natural" talents — for example, a big voice, clear diction, ease with physical movements, and thinking on their feet. The great ones develop through a will to improve and perfect their craft, through feedback, advanced training, and practice.

And so it is with great actors. However, there is one area where the traditions of the classroom and the stage differ remarkably, for teachers are, we believe, handicapped by their historic isolation from each other. By contrast, central to the tradition of the stage is the direction/rehearsal process, where every performer undergoes regular practice under the watchful eye of the director or choreographer.

As you read this book, you will find numerous exhortations from us about the benefits of feedback, support, and assistance from peers and others. As performers expect of the theatre audience, we hope you can "suspend your own disbelief" and, at the very least, experiment with some of the ideas we offer.

Cross-Fertilization and Creativity

In addition to the above, we believe that looking at your teaching through the eyes of the performer will give you some fresh insights and a wealth of ideas for improvement. The study of creativity, for instance, demonstrates the benefits of cross-fertilization and incubation. Breakthroughs often result when the mind's focus is elsewhere: Jean Piaget developed his notions of a developmental hierarchy in learning and cognition after formal studies in biology and philosophy, James Watson came to his groundbreaking work in behavioral psychology from a career in business, and Albert Einstein wrote some of his most important papers in mathematics while working at the patent office in Vienna.

Plan of This Book

We begin your journey with a contrast that both teachers and actors must face between the requirements for planning and the requirements for performance. Each must do substantial amounts of "homework" and this demands one set of skills — i.e., research, study, organization, and preparation. Yet, in class and on stage, other skills become crucial. We want to help you see the parallels.

Then we want to revisit both the lecture and the discussion as mainstays of instruction in higher education. Here we think that there are a number of lessons from the stage that can guide you toward fresh ideas for engaging students fully, for challenging them to think, to consider new possibilities, and to develop new skills.

In chapter four we explore energy, creativity, and spontaneity, qualities central to the vitality of instruction. Again, there are lessons here from the stage that can help you improve. While much has been written about the value of behavioral objectives for teachers, precious little is available to guide teachers toward more subjective qualities. In the following two chapters we make new arguments for the place of "drama" in both the development of thinking and discovery learning. Finally, we offer a range of exercises and scenes for study, to provide you with material for ongoing practice.

Come along, then! The curtain is going up! We can guarantee you'll find the journey challenging and rewarding, much like the ideal classroom experience we all want for our students. Enjoy!

Chapter 2
Warming Up

Few teachers take any time to warm up before class. Trained to be experts in content, most concentrate on the information they are bringing and, accordingly, neglect other elements that could add immeasurably to their classes. An adequate warm-up can make a difference in how you approach a class, in how you teach as well as in how your students learn. You can also lessen the likelihood of vocal strain. Moreover, a few minutes of stretching and humming can be both energizing and relaxing, giving you a few minutes to think about your students, your goals, and the rhythm you want that day. Knowing how much their performances depend on physical and mental preparation, performers are usually very disciplined about exercise, conditioning, and warm-ups.

As with athletes, warming up has long been integral to the training, practice, and performances of actors, dancers, vocalists, and musicians. Typically, actors are expected to arrive at the theatre some 50 to 60 minutes before the curtain rises, to have adequate time to warm up. For musicals and operas, leading actors and chorus members may gather together to stretch their bodies and voices. Because dancers have to express everything through their bodies, they may take even longer to warm up. As with teachers, the time taken for exercise can also permit a simultaneous focusing of intellect and emotions.

Along with promoting physical flexibility, warm-ups also help expand the physical and vocal range. Actors must project to be heard clearly in all corners of the theatre. They must enunciate clearly. Their voices must also reflect the emotions of their characters. Few roles are ever appropriate for a flat monotone: nothing is deadlier. And if they must sing, then it is obvious that they must be able to reach the notes with ease and accuracy. Even the best of scripts and scores can fail miserably if delivered poorly.

A few breathing and stretching exercises can give you more of the flexibility and focus you need to teach more effectively. We believe that taking some time for this can also help you enhance your sense of satisfaction in class. Certainly, teaching and learning are serious matters requiring careful planning and execution, but the energy and care you convey, the extent to which you can find personal fulfillment and enjoyment in your teaching, will be the fuel you need to inspire.

General Warm-Up Exercises

1. Sit comfortably, breathe deeply, and concentrate on your own physiology for breathing, feeling the air enter, fill your lungs, and leave. Or focus on a sound silently repeated over and over again. Or think of the color spectrum, imagining each color in turn, located somewhere between your eyes. Each of these exercises can help create that relaxed but alert state that physiologists call "alpha," where brain waves are rhythmic and synchronized. This is a mental state that many health professionals and devotees of meditation promote, especially as a therapeutic antidote to periods of high activity and stress.

2. Try neck rolls. (You may want to avoid rolling far to the back, since new evidence from physiologists has raised some concerns about this exercise, especially as people get older.) You could also try a sun salutation, a common yoga exercise, where you lie face down on the floor and slowly raise your head up by pushing off the floor with your arms, curving yourself upward until your arms, neck, and head are fully extended.

3. Warm up your mouth and face. Alternately tighten and stretch the various muscles. Wiggle your mouth in different directions. Pucker everything to kiss a prize pig at the local county fair. Open as wide as possible in feigned terror.

4. Do other stretching exercises, bending at the waist or going up on tip-toe with arms raised toward the sky, then swinging down to the

ground. Add the voice to follow your lifts and bends. Do this at work with your office door open and enjoy the reactions of those passing by.

Note: See the chapter, Performance-Enhancing Exercises, for an extensive description of additional exercises and activities.

For your voice, a few minutes of warm-up can help you improve your projection, variety, enunciation, intonation, and inflection. Add some understanding, training, experimentation, practice, feedback, and concentration — and who knows what you could do!

Vocal Warm-Up Exercises

Note: Some of the following exercises essentially repeat others described in this text, but with some modifications or additions specifically for the voice.

1. The musculature in your jaw, throat, face, lungs, and diaphragm combine to determine the.sounds that you can make. Rotate your neck and head. Feel the tension leave and your muscles relax. Tighten and relax the different muscle groups in your face, neck, shoulders, and stomach.

2. Now go up on your toes with your hands above your head. Stretch to the sky with your hands and let your voice push against the top of your range. Now swing your arms down to the floor as you bend your knees while your voice drops to its lowest note, then repeat several times.

3. With your hands above your head, bend left then right, forward then back. Try a "whooshing" sound as your breath comes in and out. Any sound will do.

4. Wiggle and waggle your lower jaw. (Lots of articulation problems stem from lazy jaws.) Try a tongue twister or two:

> Sally sells sea shells by the sea shore.
>   *or*
> Did a big black bug bite a big black bear?
> If a big black bug bit a big black bear,

Where is the big black bear that the big black bug
   bit?
   or
Betty Bota bought some butter
But, said she, this butter's bitter.
If I put it in my batter,
it will make my batter bitter.
So she bought some better butter,
and she put it in her batter,
and it made her batter better.

Now give your tongue a good shaking. (It's really fun to have permission to do these kinds of strange things. Blame us for any questions others may raise about propriety ... or your sanity, for that matter!)

5. Repeat the following sound combinations:
   brrrrrr ...
   ta ta ta ta ...
   me me me me ...
   us us us us ...
   la la la la ...
   ha ha ha ha ...
   bee boy by beau boo ...
   dee day die doe do ...

Now do these at different rates and with different pitches, inflections, and intonations.

6. Work on breath control. Take an eye dropper, remove the rubber cap, and inhale and exhale deeply and slowly through the little tube. Take as much time as you can with the exhaling. Do this five times a day, every day. In a week or two, your lung capacity will improve.

7. Work on "backing up" your words; have the energy and force come from the throat. Open up and relax your throat. Something to remember is that the throat is most relaxed and open during and just after a yawn. (The next time you're bored to tears in a meeting, blame us if you have to yawn.)

8. Be a bear and bellow deeply, clearing your throat. Feel your chords resonate. Get acquainted with the range of your voice; it's greater than you think.

9. Take an introduction to one of your upcoming lectures and sing it. (No, we're not trying to embarrass you!) Try moving around and adding gestures. Ham it up and really belt it out. This is a great way to explode any tendency you might have to use a monotone. After surviving this, adding a few theatrics in class will seem easy. This exercise can also help you overcome any of your blocks and get psyched for class. (If you're worried about your image, say it's an exotic Eastern ritual to focus intellectual energy! You may still want to shut the door when you do this, in case there are some around who just won't understand.)

10. Finally, consider taking the plunge and joining a choir or auditioning for a play or musical. You can learn a lot and have a great deal of fun along the way. A whole new world of possibilities may open up for you. You can experiment with ideas and techniques that have helped performers throughout the ages.

Some kind of physical warm-ups may also become increasingly important as you get older and find your joints getting stiffer. Throughout the day, and especially right before class, you may find that a few stretching exercises will feel wonderful and help reenergize your entire body. Remember: your enthusiasm in class can be very infectious.

Exercises for Physical Flexibility and Control

1. Become more aware of your posture. Stand erect, feet shoulder-width apart, knees slightly bent. Keep your head up and your eyes looking out. Try to be relaxed and alert.

2. Start with your arms stretched out to the sides, parallel to the floor. Rotate your arms from your shoulders in large circles. Now again in small circles. Rotate from the wrists, clockwise and then counter-clockwise. Try rotating your arms in opposite directions. Now try your wrists. This kind of exercise requires a kind of bodily

concentration that has wonderful payoffs on stage, especially when small, subtle movements are necessary. You may find similar benefits for your teaching.

3. Now the neck. Move your head in a large circle, first one way and then the other. Feel the tension begin to evaporate. You'll be amazed at the versatility a loose neck can provide for a whole range of characterizations, moods, or feelings. Once relaxed, you'll be better prepared for any tension that begins to build. Ask a massage therapist how important a relaxed neck is to the total relaxation of the body. Better yet, treat yourself to a massage. You deserve it!

4. Now, bend from the waist. First bend to the left, left arm by your side, right arm curved above your head and to the left. Shift your weight to the right so that you stretch your left leg. Just hang there. Don't bounce — relax! Now, center your weight and slowly bend your upper torso forward, both arms hanging down. With each exhalation you should feel yourself sinking slowly into the floor. Remember to keep your knees slightly bent. Now, swing over to the right with your left arm hooked over your head and your right arm down by your side. Shift your body weight to the left so that your right leg gets a good stretch. Finally, center your weight and bend backward, arms comfortably at your side. These kinds of stretches help release tensions that build up in your back and spine in particular, tensions that commonly result from long hours at a desk or hunched over a terminal.

5. Finally, shake your arms and legs. Pretend that you're trying to throw away a hand or a foot.

6. Before the semester begins, and especially if you are assigned to a new room, explore your teaching space. Try out your new and expanded repertoire: shout, use a stage whisper, make sounds at the top of your vocal range and then at the bottom. How do you sound in the middle of the class, at the back, on either side? Now get physical. Jump around in mock frustration tearing at your hair. Run from one side to another to celebrate an imagined superb response from a student. Skip wildly to show your childlike exuberance over a delightful solution.

Now visualize yourself performing in your classroom. See yourself in the various roles you want. Incorporate this into your regular pre-class ritual to reinforce the behaviors you want yourself to develop. (*Note:* Having survived some of these stranger recommendations, adding a little zip or something unusual to class will seem easy. Your inhibitions will have retreated in the face of your new derring-do. There is a method to this semi-madness!)

Like the actor, you need to be alert and focused to teach well. Carrying into the classroom concerns that don't belong there — a deadline hanging over your head or the residue from a contentious faculty meeting — can interfere with your concentration. Physical relaxation exercises, such as those described above, can help you cleanse your mind and body of unwanted distractions.

Some performers also use visualization exercises. For example, you might put into an imaginary box the problems you don't want to bring into the classroom. You can deal with them later! Or you can put any unwanted voices onto an imaginary tape or compact disc. Turn up the volume so that you hear the voices clearly, then slowly turn it down until you can't hear them at all. When you're ready to work, stash this recording with all those old dusty records in your basement.

Warming Up Exercise

This involves attitude as well as concentration. Here's another exercise:

1. Get up and walk around the room. As you walk, imagine that with each step you take your whole body is getting heavier: your head is growing heavier, your shoulders, your feet, your hips, your arms ... With each step, your whole body gets heavier and heavier, until it takes a great effort to move at all, yet you keep moving. (Another Monday morning!)

2. And now, imagine that with each step you take your whole body is getting lighter, lighter with each step, until you reach your normal weight. And you keep walking. (You just got that promotion!)

3. And now with each step, you continue to get lighter, lighter, and still lighter. Your arms become lighter, your head becomes lighter, your hips, your feet, your shoulders ... Now your feet are barely skimming the ground, as you become lighter and lighter. (Maybe you did inhale!)

4. And now, imagine that as you continue walking you become a little heavier with each step, until you reach your normal weight. (Uh-oh, you hear a noise outside the door!)

Take a few moments to reflect on what you experienced during the exercise. Which feeling did you prefer — heavier or lighter? Did you experience any change in mood or emotions as you became heavier? As you became lighter?

Warming Up for Class

Many people who do the above exercise report sensations of tiredness, sadness, or depression when they were "heavy." Conversely, "lightness" often stimulates feelings of happiness and freedom. As an acting exercise, this demonstrates in a very basic way the body-mind connection and what actors call the "outside-in" approach to acting.

In the "inside-out" approach, an actor studies a character's motivation and then allows what the character is thinking and feeling to produce the physical characterization "naturally." In the "outside-in" approach, the actor chooses a physical characterization and then allows the physicalization to produce the character's emotional state. For instance, an "outside-in" actor who is playing a depressed character might choose to move in a "heavy" way, while an actor playing a cheerful character might choose a "light" movement pattern. The actor is not just "pretending" to be depressed or cheerful — the movement pattern itself can stimulate the desired feelings.

Evaluation forms often ask students to comment on their teacher's enthusiasm for the subject matter. Certainly, your sincere interest in the subject communicates itself to students. But the most enthusiastic of us encounter days when we're grumpy and just "not in the mood" for class. An attitude warm-up can help get you in the mood, whether you choose an "inside-out" approach of positive self-talk or an "outside-in" approach of deliberately changing your movement patterns. The point is that you can choose your attitude — if you remember to do so and take the time to warm up. If you choose to move in a more lively and energetic pattern, you should feel more lively and energetic.

Exercises like those described here can help you set a more positive physical, mental, and emotional tone for yourself. In the midst of your regular routines and pressures, taking some time to get ready for your classes may seem like a luxury you cannot afford. However, if you come to enjoy this kind of preparation, your teaching can really improve. If you feel more energized, your students should respond accordingly. If you are more focused, your teaching can be more focused. Indeed, these effects can be quite interactive: a synergism can develop between you and your students that can make teaching feel more rewarding and your classes more enjoyable, for you and your students.

Chapter 3
Planning
and Performance

One of the most challenging aspects of higher education requires teachers to be skillful in both planning and performance, in their preparation of clear and organized notes for class as well as in their behavior in the classroom. The contrasts between these two areas is striking. While planning requires study and quiet reflection, teaching is active and interactive, often pressured. While planning builds upon years of schooling and experience, teaching is focused on the present and must accommodate a wide range of factors, from the expected to the unpredictable, from student needs to classroom conditions to audiovisual equipment.

For example, student questions and comments can run the gamut from the predictable — "Will this be on the exam?" — to the personal — "What do you think?" — to the blunt — "Do we have to come to class?" In many classrooms, chairs are bolted to the floor, but in some you may find the chairs scattered all over the place or the floor littered with newspapers, soda cans, and such. You may have a day when you've got to scrap your plans because the equipment you'd planned to use malfunctions.

Again, there are very real contrasts between planning and performance at play here. Most teachers work quite independently on their plans for class, often in their offices, at home, or in the library. Yet, teaching itself is highly interdependent, a function of your relationships with your students and the learning experiences you can create.

While planning is quite private, teaching is very intensely public, with increasingly critical audiences. While you may be very flexible about when, where, and how you plan, you must meet your classes at set times. The show must go on. In many ways, planning enables you to conceptualize and manage your classes effectively, especially in large classes, for which you may need to supervise teaching assistants or coordinate the use of guest lecturers and the grading of exams.

In sum, successful teaching requires skill in both planning and performance. You must come prepared as the expert, yet also prepared to think on your feet. Unfortunately, we who teach in higher education rarely receive formal training in the performance aspects of our teaching. Since actors, dancers, and singers come from a tradition that systematically addresses both planning and performance, we believe that their world can offer you new insights, concrete techniques, and creative ideas for translating your subject matter expertise into dynamic, engaging instruction.

In this chapter, we only want to touch upon these lessons and try to help you become more aware. In later chapters, we will go into greater depth.

Performers begin to plan long before a production opens. Once casting is completed, formal rehearsals begin and preparation becomes ncreasingly intense. Even for non-professional productions, it takes about six weeks to get everything in place and refined. Because most performers are obligated to families and to jobs (only 55% of performers are paid as professionals), they must squeeze three to four hours out of their evenings and weekends for rehearsals, with even more time needed closer to opening.

That's a very heavy investment of time and energy, so performers know that they must work to attract and hold their audiences. How demoralizing to put countless hours and a lot of work into a production and then play to a dead audience or an empty house! Performances must be lively and inspired when so much is at stake.

Similarly, teachers in higher education begin planning long before a course begins — researching material, selecting a text or creating a class reader, outlining assignments, and matching dates and deadlines with the campus calendar. We work hard to prepare for our courses, so we should work hard to make our classes lively and inspired, to derive the best results from our preparation.

Given the importance of planning and psychological preparation for your teaching, we want to draw on our experiences with performers to offer the following suggestions:

- Be aware of the conditions that allow you to be most productive when planning.

- Schedule time to review past classes and to think about what you will do the next time.

- Take a few minutes before each class and focus on your physical readiness with some simple exercises to boost your heart rate.

- You could quietly recall moments when you felt especially excited about the material, paying careful attention to the details of those memories, to the classroom, your actions, even your attire. As you re-experience these moments, note the accompanying feelings and try to bring these with you to class.

- Put reminders in your notes to be energetic, move more, or stir up a lively discussion.

- Get to the classroom early and set up, so that you can begin class right on time. Convey a sense of urgency about what you want to accomplish, about doing all that you have planned.

- Be ambitious about what you want to accomplish each class period, so that your high expectations also fuel your own sense of urgency.

- Observe other classes and chat with colleagues about their approaches to preparation and performing.

Warm-Up

For the actor, getting ready for a role or even for rehearsal is quite different from getting ready for a performance. When planning, the actor must research the character, speculating about possible motivations or relationships with the other characters, and learn lines. Once the production is at hand, warm-up becomes much more serious, intense, focused. Here, actors must make a conscious transition into the characters they will portray. This inevitably requires intellectual, emotional, and physical warm-up. Most actors find it essential to use the "green room" behind a stage to concentrate, to begin moving and interacting in character, to review lines and cues.

Although you may not think of them as warm-ups, you probably have your own idiosyncratic routines that help you prepare and perform. What we will discuss here is not a repeat of earlier material, but rather a new way to frame your approach to these areas.

When planning, for example, you may reserve certain days and times for writing at home or for research at the library. You may need quiet and focus to be most productive. You may need your references, your word processor, or a copy machine close at hand. Like many of us, you may need at least one good cup of coffee to get going.

You warm up in quite different ways for teaching. You may like to review your notes right up until class, spending most of your time on the content, trying to get the wording just right or the material to fit within the allotted time period. You probably take little if any time for emotional or physical preparation.

From our experiences with performers, we can suggest the following ideas for warming up to teach:

- Be aware of what you need to be efficient, productive, and creative, whether you are preparing material or getting ready to teach.

- Review the names of your students, so that your class can have a more personal feel. If the class is large, remind yourself to learn a few more names each day. Use the names you know: a periodic roll call not only lets you know who is present but also gives you a chance to practice names.

- Reflect some about the dynamics of previous classes and what you could do differently.

- Put your notes aside and get physically ready for class. As we have already noted earlier, a few stretching exercises can do wonders to loosen muscles and release pent-up tension. Humming can warm up your voice so that you minimize strain and are primed to provide more vocal variety. A favorite song can help lift your mood and improve your frame of mind. Just whistle while you work!

Lesson Plans and Scripts

You write your notes in advance of class, just as scripts are secured long before any "performance." However, teachers have a wonderful advantage here, because they are free to alter their plans at any moment, to pick up on a particularly good question, to review a troubling concept or spark a discussion, to tie into something in the news that day. Consequently, they must come to class fully prepared but ever alert to student needs, in much the same way that actors work with improvisation. Here, your expertise and preparation combine to allow you to respond knowingly in the moment.

Yet, even here we believe that there are useful lessons to draw from the stage. First, to perform well, actors must memorize their lines and cues. Second, performers often make extensive use of the margins of their scripts for notes and reminders to themselves. Third, actors must also take time to get into character, to prepare physically and emotionally as well as to review the script. Otherwise, productions may be wooden, a series of recited lines and memorized actions that don't feel real to the audience.

For teachers, then, we offer the following recommendations:

- Know your material well enough to be able to address your students directly and make eye contact. This will allow you to notice those who seem lost or who may be drifting off. This will also free you from the podium and permit you to roam freely around the room. Being closer to your students can make a difference. If you overlearn your material, you enjoy greater freedom to create spontaneous and engaging learning experiences.

- Leave wide margins on your notes so that you can jot reminders to yourself.

- Put your plans aside as class time approaches and allow yourself a few moments to concentrate on getting physically and emotionally ready.

- Reflect on what you do differently. Check with students about their reactions. Plan to allow these changes a longer run, to see how effective they are over several class sessions. Much in the theatre involves trial and error; performers learn quickly to be aggressive about taking risks.

Roles

For both teachers and performers, what is necessary to prepare for a production may be quite different from what is required once class begins or the curtain rises. When getting ready, study, reflection, and training are necessary. In class or on stage, however, very different roles come into play.

The role demands for teachers in class are extensive, varied, complex, and ever changing, shifting, and blending. Because you have to determine grades, you play the judge. When you handle all the attendant logistical decisions, you play the manager. When students are in crisis, you may play the counselor. When students struggle to understand despite your best efforts, you may have to shift gears, to play magician and pull something new out of your hat.

What we can recommend from our experiences on the stage are as follows:

- Be conscious of the roles you must play. Awareness alone can make a difference. Perhaps different hats, real or just imagined, can help you shift as required. Each role may have a different look and emotion — a "thinking" hat, perhaps a different one for writing, another that lets you perform well in front of groups, and yet another for facilitating group discussions. Taking the use of the "thinking" or "writing" hat quite literally may help you better protect the time you want to set aside for these activities. These kinds of "costuming cues" may help you stay focused as well as signal others when you are busy and thus not available.

- Talk with respected colleagues about the roles they play. Observe them in their classes.

- Write out the requirements for your roles, so that you can be more clear and focused about each.

- Seek feedback from others, colleagues and students in particular, about how effectively you play each of your various roles.

- Read. Take classes. Join relevant discussion groups on the Internet. Make your own professional and personal development a high priority. Invest in yourself.

Movements and Blocking

Your movements — or lack thereof — constitute what the performer calls "blocking." The blocking required for a stage production is carefully plotted far in advance, refined in rehearsal, and then practiced until all movements appear easy and natural. Then, once the curtain lifts, directors and actors expect to remain faithful to their plans. There will be no place for spontaneous improvisation; in fact, everyone involved commits to "no surprises." Errors can be understood, but unnecessary improvisation only makes everyone crazy.

In the classroom, what you do physically can support or undermine what you say and thereby affect what and how your students learn. However, preparing for this and following through can be two very different challenges.

Before class begins, you can make notations about blocking in the margins of your class notes. For instance, if you are trying to add a bit of variety and break your dependence on the lectern, you can remind yourself to move toward a student who raises a question. You might create a more personalized conversation this way. If a discussion develops, you might want to move to the middle of the room.

Note the different "feel" when you do this. Reflect on it. Put your thoughts in writing. What do students think? Ask them. Or take a few minutes and have them write their reactions on a piece of paper. You will benefit from the feedback and they will appreciate your concern. Indeed, we believe that this interest in feedback is one of the major lessons teachers can draw from the stage.

That's the planning side of it. Now, what happens once class begins? There are times when you will have to leave your prepared notes and interact more spontaneously. Here you can discipline yourself to be more aware of your movements and how they may affect your students. You develop a split consciousness that allows you to watch yourself while you teach, a skill that performers must hone to be successful on stage. With training, experience, practice, and concentration, actors can become quite proficient here — and so can you.

For example, you can never predict exactly when or where questions will arise. Indeed, you may want to stimulate questions at certain points or encourage students who rarely participate. Your movements can make a difference here. You may spark more engagement from some students by getting physically closer to them. Being closer may also allow you to notice subtle reactions, confusion, or agreement and pull more students into the discussion. You can also become more aware of times when you might be obstructing someone's view. If you are usually up in front and focused on your notes, varying your movements can provide some variety and relief.

Equipment and Materials as Props

Actors and directors must think through any props they want to use and work them very carefully so that each adds something to the performance. Again, although performers need to learn how to think on their feet when someone makes a mistake, misses a cue, or mislays a prop — the show must go on! — there should never be any random, spontaneous use of props on stage.

When you plan your class, consider the equipment, materials, and other items that can be useful, that can help illustrate certain concepts or function as catalysts for learning activities. From pointers to big chalk for a large lecture hall, from slides to videos, from transparencies to materials for demonstrations, these "props" can have a very positive impact on learning. It's important to plan carefully to be sure you have at hand what you need.

However, once class begins, you will also have a great deal of freedom to decide exactly when and how to use each prop. You will also have the opportunity to shift plans. (Here again, teachers have an advantage over performers.) However, you may also have to deal with surprises along the way — equipment that malfunctions, items that you forgot to bring, plans that fail for some reason. Being able to think on your feet is a skill you can cultivate with planning, awareness, experience, practice, and creative resourcefulness. Once again, feedback and risk-taking, so important on stage, become essential.

Lighting

As with props, performers must determine the exact kinds of lighting they want for which actions, which characters, and for how long. While classical musicians typically work with one set lighting pattern, rock groups often use a splashy, pulsating range of lighting options, including lasers, strobes, and whirling spots, in every color imaginable. Dancers will use light changes to support different moods and movements. At times, the late choreographer Randy Wray broke from the classical ballet tradition of constant and bright lighting to use very vivid colors to evoke particular feelings. He knew that ballet must be creative to compete for its share of attention amid all the bright and flashy entertainment options. For plays, directors may want to illuminate the entire stage at one point, but then, in the next moment, dim the lights and put one of the actors in a bright spot. A wide variety of more subtle changes, often imperceptible to those in the audience, can enhance a story as it unfolds on stage.

Teachers rarely pay much attention to lighting, so this note may seem trivial. However, there are times when your planning can make all the difference. Perhaps the sunlight might make a video nearly impossible to see and scheduling another room would make a great difference. You may already be sufficiently tuned into your students to sense when you could dim the lights and make it easier for them to see an overhead or a slide. Your students should feel comfortable enough to interrupt you if they cannot see. At the very least, you could ask them if you're unsure. If students are making presentations, you may want to take the lead in adjusting the lights, since they may not do so themselves. Varying the lighting can also help keep students alert, as the changes can recapture flagging attention.

The next time you are in a theatre or watching a movie or television, notice the effects of lighting on the story. Of course, directors work all this out in meticulous detail far in advance of the performance. While you will always want to be free to improvise in class, you may be able to resolve or avoid certain problems or create some very special moments by planning your lighting.

Costuming

Costuming is so important to a staged production, film, or video that producers go to great lengths to get it right — and getting it right often proves to be quite expensive. What fun to see a period piece come alive with fancy gowns, capes, hats, and all! All this investment can make it much easier for audiences to indulge in the "willing suspension of disbelief" and sink into a performance.

Clothing makes a difference in the classroom as well. Although that environment can feel quite informal, your clothing can have an impact. For example, a professor of sports and exercise sciences found that, when she returned exams, she could eliminate some of the complaints and hassles by wearing a suit instead of sweats. Her students seemed more likely to haggle over points with her when she dressed less formally. The interviews included in our "Foreword From the

Classroom" describe how aware two gifted teachers, biologist Janice
Moore and folklorist Carol Mitchell, are about their clothing/costuming.

As with blocking, props, and lighting, costuming for any stage production is designed long before it opens. The lessons we draw for teaching are as follows:

- Be aware of the impact of clothing in general, on others and
  on yourself, when it may be important to "look professional,"
  for example, or when formality may inhibit your creativity,
  put an unnecessary barrier between you and your students,
  or make you may feel uneasy about going outside to hold
  class on the grass when you're wearing some of your better
  clothes.

- Experiment. Test your assumptions and hypotheses about
  clothing. Check it out with others, especially students.

- Try simple "costume" changes. They can help you in various roles you may want to play in class, from debates to
  dramatizations. Although you need to plan what you want,
  you can also call on the imaginations of your students when
  you need them to "see" a certain piece of clothing, such as
  when you're discussing someone from the history of your discipline and you need to fill in some of the background details.

Energy and Concentration

For performers, the differences between what is required to prepare
for a role and what is needed on stage can be like night and day. The
progression of the rehearsal process links the two. Everyone may be
relatively calm at the outset, but emotions and focus will peak as
opening night draws closer. Once the curtain rises, everyone wants to
be alert and attentive to what is happening on stage, but relaxed and
confident in their preparation.

An important shift also happens for teachers between what they do
to prepare and what happens in class. It is the rehearsal process that
helps the performer make this kind of shift. Be aware of your energies and abilities to concentrate in class, especially since learning depends so much on the enthusiasm you bring to the material and to
your students.

As you prepare for class, you set goals, choose and organize material, and plan activities. This is the instructional equivalent of writing a play, selecting a cast, designing sets, and rehearsing.

When class begins, there's a shift. You must deal with the human elements, the unexpected, the variables of an educational environment. You've planned activities by the clock, but now you may find it helpful to monitor the reactions of your students while watching the clock. When you enter into a discussion, you don't know exactly what students will say or ask or how the focus will shift, what you will need to do to keep everyone engaged.

There are important differences between audiences in the theatre and students in a class, of course, and we don't want to minimize these. Attending a single performance is far different from working through difficult material week after week in a course. Sitting in a comfortable seat, separated from the stage, is far different from being in the midst of the classroom action.

Teachers, here again, enjoy some advantages over performers. They don't have to present the same material day after day and they really are very free to shift gears, improvise, or create something altogether new and different as necessary.

Despite these significant differences, however, we believe that teachers can profit a great deal from understanding more about the stage and about how performers sustain their energy and concentration through long performances.

Audience Response

Through experience, teachers and performers alike learn to anticipate certain reactions. However, both have to deal with an element of the unexpected as well. For example, the actor can note places where it may be important to hold a line or a gesture just a bit longer, so that the audience can get all it wants out of a situation. Similarly, you may want to note where a longer pause following a difficult question could allow more students to come up with a response.

As teachers, we enjoy an important advantage over actors, in our freedom to shift gears and spend more time with a discussion, better engage our students, or provide an impromptu explanation as necessary.

Some real examples:

- Bettina Aptheker (Women's Studies, University of California-
  Santa Cruz) often uses storytelling as a method of teaching,
  drawing up relevant experiences from her own life, or those
  of women she knows. She becomes more animated and more
  personal, adding the kind of emotion and rich
  detail that is highly engaging.

- Sandy Kern (Physics, Colorado State University) will depart
  from his plans when students appear confused. He uses common examples to make difficult concepts or principles much
  more accessible and understandable. In a very spontaneous
  way, he'll use imagery, objects, gestures, and diagrams —
  whatever comes to mind — to describe new and different
  examples. It really is demanding, he says, to do that on the
  spur of the moment when the need arises, but why press on
  when students don't get it?

- Gil Findlay (English, Colorado State University) typically
  lectures in an up-tempo manner, but regularly indulges in
  long and personal digressions to illustrate issues from the
  readings (autobiographies) or discussion. While a few students are so addicted to the extrinsic rewards and worry
  so much about their grades — e.g., required assignments
  and exams — that they get impatient with these stories,
  most thoroughly enjoy these insights into the personal life
  and thoughts of a teacher who has been a student favorite
  for years. In this way Findlay becomes more human, more
  real, less of an authority figure, someone with hopes and
  dreams, joys and tragedies, worries, good and bad days.
  Over time, and with his encouragement and modeling, students begin to shift from their preoccupation with graded
  hurdles to jump and accept the challenge and unique opportunity to look deeply within their own stories and begin to
  sort out what is most meaningful, essential, unique, or problematic.

We advise you to start with your own awareness of your students
and how their engagement affects what and how they learn. Expand
from here to experiment actively, to probe their reactions and solicit
their feedback. We'll also add more on this later.

Exercises

1. Throughout this chapter we have emphasized the importance of self-awareness as a starting point. To guide you in this process, rate your skills (circle H-High, M-Medium, or L-Low) in the following areas. Which factors affect your performance?

Planning	Rating	Comments
Library research	H M L	
Anticipating problems	H M L	
Arranging for trips, speakers, etc.	H M L	
Vocal projection	H M L	
Clarity of speech (enunciation)	H M L	
Arranging for equipment	H M L	
Enthusiasm	H M L	
Response to questions	H M L	
Facilitation of discussion	H M L	
Thinking on your feet	H M L	
Awareness of audience	H M L	
Awareness of self	H M L	
Awareness of roles	H M L	
Awareness of movements	H M L	
Awareness of props	H M L	
Awareness of lighting	H M L	
Awareness of costuming	H M L	
Awareness of energy	H M L	
Awareness of concentration	H M L	

2. Interview several colleagues about their skills in both the planning and performance aspects of teaching. Seek out those with especially good reputations as teachers. Observe them in class.

Chapter 4
The Lecture

Do you want to engage your students more enthusiastically during lecture? Do you want to feel more energized about teaching, more excited about going to class every day, and more confident that your teaching is effective, engaging, and getting better?

Although the word "lecture" is derived from the Latin word for reading, students today want and deserve much more. Besides, with the advent of desktop publishing and photocopying technologies, you can compile lecture notes to distribute or place on reserve and think instead about class in ways that are much more creative and challenging, that make much better use of available technologies, campus and community resources, and student talents.

If you want students to go beyond surface learning, to do more than memorize, to be better able to think deeply and for themselves, then you may want to consider various alternative approaches. We recognize that discovery learning and creativity training, for example, require students to be quite active in sorting through material and constructing meaning for themselves. As such we offer separate chapters on these and other approaches that have parallels to the stage. However, in this chapter, we want to address those issues that arise from lecturing.

Why Lecture?

The lecture has been a mainstay in higher education over the centuries. Its advantages are substantial. Quite simply, the lecture allows you to interject the most current thinking, long before new findings run the gauntlet of refereed research journals and appear in print. Additionally, the lecture allows you to address topical or controversial issues or refer to items that students may raise.

Perhaps as important, however, the lecture represents a very flexible administrative structure for scheduling classes and accommodating shifts in enrollments. Class size may be of little significance: it could be easy to add more students and take full advantage of all the physical space available. If the instructional paradigm is about information transmission, then even room size is no barrier, as the wonders of technology permit broadcast and access in very flexible formats.

We know, however, that for certain goals and under certain conditions other approaches to instruction can have distinct advantages. For example, technology increasingly permits much more in the way of independent and active learning, access to information and ongoing electronic interactions. Just as important are the benefits that students can derive from small group and cooperative learning, from various forms of experiential learning, or from activities that encourage critical and creative thinking and promote deeper understanding.

Yet, we also recognize the enduring utility of the lecture. And because there are such close parallels between a good performance and an engaging lecture, we will describe a number of ways in which lessons from the stage can help you energize your lectures, inspire your students, and promote learning. In this chapter, we will share ideas that can help you better prepare for your lectures and make the best use of your voice, gestures, and teaching materials. We will show you how you can improve your lectures with ideas about scripts, how you can better challenge minds and harness emotions. We will describe how training and rehearsal techniques can help make performances more believable and how knowledge about set designs and lighting can also contribute in subtle but effective ways.

The Challenge to Lecture Well

Despite the lecture's seeming simplicity, you may find this format a challenge, and especially so:

- When classes are large
- When some students show up unprepared or unmotivated

- When the material begs for interaction

- When the availability of relevant media is limited

- When there is little money for teaching assistants

- When some students seem to want to know only what will be on the next exam

- When too few are in their seats on time and too many begin to leave too soon

- When those who want to chat with friends disturb their classmates

- When the fear of public speaking rears its ugly head and shakes your confidence

We can assure you that even the best teachers share some of these same fears and frustrations. We also believe that rethinking the lecture as a stage and the class as a production can give you many fresh new ideas for meeting these challenges.

Public speaking may intimidate you. It certainly is difficult for many and terrifying for some. At the height of the Cold War, public speaking ranked first in a U.S. poll of "Greatest Fears" — even above nuclear holocaust! Others have put the resulting stress high on lists that include such personal traumas as divorce, loss of employment, and death of loved ones. Even for extroverts, a public talk can be a challenge, especially when the group is large or intimidating.

As difficult for you, however, may be the tension that students create when they demand simple truths or want only what can be expected on the next exam! If you are actively involved in research, you know the frustration when you are asked to reduce the most tentative understandings of complex matters into 50-minute lectures that make note-taking easy. If you labor to convey the essence of your subject, if you want students to leave with a deep understanding, then you probably feel frustrated when some exhibit a constant concern about requirements and grading.

In this era of fast-paced media images, how can you ever hope to capture and hold the attention of your students for an hour or more with just your own descriptions, explanations, and ideas? When film and television production require so much money, expertise, and equipment, how can you ever hope to compete on your own? If you are well trained with a great deal of experience to share, you may feel

quite uncomfortable with the limitations and demands of the lecture
format, especially in large and diverse classes. You may also agree
with criticisms that the lecture focuses too much on knowledge transmission and limits active and experiential learning opportunities.

Lessons from the Stage

A lecturer who stands rooted at a podium and drones on and on in a
dry and uninspired monotone can rarely inspire. In contrast, nearly
everyone has memories of riveting speakers. Those of us who teach
understand that the effective use of posture, voice, gestures, timing,
and the like can make lectures more interesting and effective and
help us engage our students intellectually and emotionally.

Ken Klopfenstein (Mathematics, Colorado State University) is a good
example of a gifted lecturer who makes the most of class time. He is
focused and organized, but friendly and flexible. He moves through
material efficiently, but pauses frequently to make sure that his students understand, to allow them to think and ask questions. He
moves across the front of the classroom, stopping periodically to emphasize key points. What is truly remarkable is the way in which he
will build suspense as he works through a particular problem or proof
and, at times, reach a resolution in the final minute of class. And in
linear algebra, mind you! From a theatre perspective, there is much
to applaud here — and much for any teacher to emulate.

However, you may not feel confident in your abilities to harness
those powers of delivery. We believe that you can learn a great deal
from the stage to enhance your preparation and performance, to help
you transform your lecture notes into scripts that energize and inspire.

The Teaching Objective
as Through-Line

Good lecturing is a high-wire juggling act. You enter the room with
certain expectations. You know what you want to cover. However,
you must simultaneously be aware of the conditions you face in any
particular class, the mechanics of getting class started and ended on
time, of using the board or various pieces of equipment. While doing
all that, you must also be thinking forward and preview upcoming
events — exams, papers, field trips, guest lecturers, demonstrations

— in a timely manner. You also have to think about learning objectives, what you hope that your students will be able to understand and do, and about Plan B or Plan C in case Plan A doesn't work.

We believe that, if you could listen more closely to your students, to their struggles and needs, you would be able to give greater attention to the framework and the threads that help them connect the facts, figures, and details of the course material to underlying core concepts. Because plays and movies are carefully constructed, because every line, action, and gesture is connected to a central theme, we think that they provide valuable lessons for structuring your lectures.

Of course, our lectures are not stage performances. We rarely repeat our lectures: we change and update our notes, we face different questions, we enter into digressions. Few of us have the occasion, then, or the time and incentive to work on our performances in ways that parallel how playwrights polish their scripts and actors perfect their roles. However, we can make our lectures as effective as possible, whatever our circumstances. If a play flops, the members of an audience go home disappointed, having wasted a few hours and some money. However, what is the cost to students when their teachers leave them confused or overwhelmed by facts to be simply memorized? How much better when you can help your students connect their learning to the underlying structure of a discipline! Performing artists have something important here to share with teachers.

Every play and movie has an objective or *through-line* that plays out through the characters, the action, and the plot. In *Death of a Salesman*, Willy Loman has to confront his own limitations and, ultimately, learns to accept his place in the world. Macbeth has to reconcile his own evil after killing his king. In *Field of Dreams*, Shoeless Joe Jackson and his teammates return from the grave to play again, when the Kevin Costner character has built the ballpark. Just ask yourself, would audiences have paid to see Thelma and Louise stop their car and just give up?

Directors and actors trained in the Stanislavski tradition term the unifying element of a script the play's *spine*. Harold Clurman (1972, 27-28), a major American director, explains:

> To begin active direction a formulation in the simplest terms must be found to state what general action motivates the play, of what fundamental drama or conflict the script's plot and people are the instruments. ...

Many things are contained in O'Neill's *Desire Under the Elms*: passion, Oedipal impulses, confessions of unhappiness and hate, guilt feelings, paternal harshness, filial vindictiveness, retribution. But what holds all these ingredients together, what makes a complete meaning, a single specific drama of them all, is the play's spine.

The director analyzes the play in terms of the spine, defining for each character a spine — a main action or objective, stated as an infinitive verb — that shows how that character relates to the main action of the play. "Where such a relation is not evident or non-existent," Clurman (1972, 74) points out, "the character performs no function in the play."

Just as a play or film or novel needs a clear storyline or through-line or spine, so does a lecture. Your message must have a clear organizing purpose. Just as all of the character spines must relate to the play spine, all of the elements of your lecture should help you achieve your primary objective of organizing material to help your students learn more effectively.

Try analyzing one of your lectures as if it were a play script. What is the spine? How does the spine communicate the theme, the meaning, of the lecture? What are the spines of the various parts of the lecture? How do they relate to the primary spine? Will students follow the connections?

Such detailed attention to preparing a lecture requires a considerable investment of time, of course. Although rewards for research and publications on some campuses may lead many of us to question this kind of commitment to teaching, it offers considerable benefits for our students and all those intrinsic rewards we get from a job well done. (Moreover, colleagues and administrators always appreciate the skillful lecturer who can successfully handle large numbers of students.)

There are also benefits for you outside the classroom. These skills obviously transfer easily to professional presentations that you might make at conferences and elsewhere. The careful attention that you devote to your lecture "scripts" may help you, for example, convert your notes and presentations into published papers, chapters, and books. Perhaps you might also want to write about innovations that you've tried in teaching, where some of these lessons from the stage have made a real impact. Boyer's (1990) groundbreaking report for the Carnegie Commission on Higher Education, *The Professoriate Reconsidered*, makes a very articulate call to expand the notion of scholarship, to recognize more than just basic research and to rebalance our reward systems to promote higher-quality instruction.

No matter how well you lecture, though, we urge you not to neglect opportunities to interact with your students. You can maximize these opportunities by reducing the material burden on your lectures. As resources and systems allow, you can package materials as handouts, put them on reserve in the library, include them in a course reader for sale through the bookstore, or make them available for students to copy. Then, think about ways to use class time more creatively.

Here is where the lecture has distinct advantages over the written script. From questions and brief discussions to spontaneous digressions, from debates to group evaluations of relevant cases, you can always spice up your lectures with new and topical material and energize your students with periodic activities. In essence, you can use your written notes as a platform for opportunities to engage your students more actively in deeper learning.

Exercises

As we wrote in the introduction, the world of performance arts can stimulate our thinking about creative alternatives to traditional teaching methods. Although the following exercises focus on staged productions, we believe that they will give you some fresh insights into your teaching.

1. Analyze a favorite play, film, or television program. Determine what you think the through-line or spine might be — what holds it all together, the main action. What is the theme of the piece? How does the spine point to the theme? See if, for each of the major characters, you can identify spines that relate to the main spine. Watch or read the piece again, noting how the dialogue and actions fit the spines.

Learning to recognize spines takes practice. If you have difficulty, try a preliminary step: state the main action of the play in a single sentence (called a *root action*). The root action statement has the following parts:

- A description of the protagonist

- A description of the main action the protagonist takes during the play

- A description of the result of that action

Thus the statement takes the form: "This is a play about a _____ who _____ and thereby _____." Since the spine of a play relates closely to the spine of the protagonist, a clear root action statement will help you discover what the playwright is doing in the play — its spine.

2. Reflect on one of your recent lectures. Was the spine clear to the students? The theme? Find a few students to ask. How might you apply your knowledge of play construction to improve the lecture?

Lecture Notes as Script

In addition to the underlying objective or through-line, the notes you prepare for your lecture resemble scripts in other ways. Essentially, they organize information and ideas around your central themes in a logical way that your students will understand. You can include notes about delivery as well, perhaps in the margins, similar to stage directions in a script. For example, you can make reminders for yourself to pause at certain points, to ask questions or solicit comments, to call on particular students, or to just allow your students time to reflect.

Instructors at the post-secondary level rarely receive formal training in lecturing skills. Playwrights, on the other hand, can go through years of intensive study and practice, a tradition dating from the earliest Greek theatre. Accordingly, much is known about writing successful scripts — and, we believe, a lot of that knowledge can be useful for teachers.

Scholars of drama consider conflict the heart of drama. A play without conflict proves boring. Conflicts engage audience interest and generate suspense. How will the conflict be resolved? Who will win? Who loses? The hero's journey has always been complicated by obstacles, problems, uncertainty, challenges — real tests of character. In the theatre, there are three levels of conflicts: conflicts between individuals, conflicts within an individual, and conflicts between an individual and larger forces (nature, society, fate, etc.). The great plays, those that continue to appeal to generations of audiences, often include all three levels of conflict.

When scripting your lecture, look for opportunities to emphasize the conflicts inherent in the material. Presenting a string of facts challenges your students far less than showing them how knowledge often conflicts with ignorance, beliefs, and assumptions.

Strange or paradoxical phenomena can make for wonderful study. Researchers working in basic mathematics have long studied what may seem to many others to be the most esoteric problems. Where will the next discoveries come in chemistry? Physics seems full of oddities with theories about black holes, quarks, and relativity — and the very nature of the universe — pushing the limits of our understanding.

Consider how the environment defies traditional ways of thinking. Despite massive amounts of data and the most powerful supercomputers, our ability to predict the weather using conventional approaches has proven quite limited. Thus evolved "chaos theory" and hypotheses about nonlinear relationships, where a small change in temperature could dramatically affect overall weather patterns because of the interplay of many other variables. Are there areas within your own discipline where ideas may be counterintuitive?

Ethical issues exist in every discipline and present many opportunities for addressing conflict. Here, you can always ask your students to consider the problems that arise when scholars critique prevailing theories and propose new perspectives. The history of science, for example, is full of stories about races between individuals or labs to be the first to announce a particular discovery. The film, *And the Band Played On,* depicts one such competition between an American and a French lab to discover a viable test for HIV (AIDS). At the time, the death toll from this mysterious disease was ravaging gay communities in particular; panic and fear were mixing with public apathy and resistance in a very deadly brew. By ignoring breakthroughs from the Americans and waiting for their own scientists, senior officials in the French ministry of health allowed blood supplies tainted with HIV to go out unscreened. High stakes and high drama!

Managed effectively, conflicts can certainly help students clarify their own values. In our chapter on making the developmental case for drama, we describe in great detail how teachers can use dilemmas as catalysts for stimulating growth in moral development. For example, you might explore issues like cheating or plagiarism with a hypothetical case study. You can ask students to judge a particular behavior and then probe their reasoning for the underlying values.

"What if" questions can help you identify the conditions that determine the boundaries of student values, when cooperation becomes cheating and paraphrasing becomes plagiarism. Open discussions in class can provide the kind of rich interaction of values and reasoning that stimulates students to reflect and grow ... and you simultaneously address an issue relevant to the integrity of your class.

The study of conflict in the theatre can offer other insights into teaching. In the 4th century B.C., Aristotle argued in his *Poetics* that action is the most significant element of drama and that playwrights must structure the action of their plays with great care. A play opens with some situation, called the *stasis* or *balance*, that contains the potential for significant action. Through exposition — background information essential to understanding the stasis — the audience gradually senses the instability in the situation, the potential for action.

An *inciting incident*, an event that disrupts the tenuous balance, sets in motion the main action of the play. A protagonist, the play's central character, sets out on a course of action in order to achieve a goal. In the course of pursuing that goal, the protagonist encounters a series of complications, events, or factors that help or hinder him or her and thus build suspense. Most plays contain a *major crisis*, a *turning point* when the protagonist must make a choice that will eventually determine the outcome of the play.

Throughout the play, the author creates an *emotional rhythm*, structuring the emotional dynamics so as to build to high points of tension and suspense, *climaxes* that are usually followed by periods of relative relaxation. In the overall rhythm, the author progressively builds emotional involvement up to the major emotional climax. Then, in a single moment, the author resolves the play's main action and delineates a new stasis or balance.

The *thematic significance*, the *meaning* of a play, arises from its action. What action does the playwright choose to represent? What forces are in conflict? What choices do the characters make, especially the protagonist? Why do they make these choices? What happens to them as a result of their choices? What insights about human life can we, the audience, get from the vicarious experience provided by the play?

Not all lectures lend themselves to this kind of design, of course. But drama has long served as a teaching tool in various disciplines. The Roman poet Horace pointed out that the purpose of drama is not only to entertain but to instruct. Of course, some of the greatest teachers have been great storytellers. Jesus of Nazareth relied much on the parable, a type of short story, to communicate his ideas. Plato related the teachings of his mentor Socrates in the form of written dialogues — plays! On campus today — and especially in certain applied disciplines, such as law, business, and the health sciences — entire courses may evolve from discussions of cases or problems.

Study of the playwright's methods for engaging attention and interest can help you better structure your lectures. For instance, you can learn to adapt playwrighting techniques for building to a climax (to emphasize major points) and then, following the emotional rhythm, allow a period of relative relaxation (so students can assimilate new material) before beginning another build.

Research on learning reveals a distinct pattern, in which students forget more material from the middle of lectures than at the beginning or end. At the beginning of class, students are fresh; there is little *proactive interference* from earlier material. At the end of class, memories are fresh because there is no later material to cause *retroactive interference*. You can do much to help your students retain more from the middle of your lectures. You can refer to the underlying concepts more frequently to facilitate organization of memory. You can keep your objectives for a particular class on the board or overhead as a reference throughout the class period. You can intersperse brief written or oral activities for students throughout your lecture as buffers to interference and as a help for consolidating learning. You can use more concrete examples.

In addition, you can apply the concept of the major dramatic question to your lectures. Here, we can look at an extended example from the theatre. The inciting incident raises a major dramatic question for the audience, a question about the outcome of the play. Interest in discovering the answer to this question helps keep the audience attentive to the performance. Read on and see if this technique could work for you.

The Case of Oedipus

In *Oedipus the King*, Sophocles presents a stasis in which a plague has been devastating Thebes. In the opening scene, citizens plead with Oedipus to save the city from the plague; Oedipus replies that he has sent his brother-in-law Creon to ask the oracle for advice. Creon returns with the oracle's message: the plague is to punish the city for harboring the murderer of Laius, the previous king. Creon's announcement (the inciting incident) prompts Oedipus (the protagonist) to set off on a quest to find the murderer (main action), thus posing the major dramatic question: Will Oedipus find the murderer?

(Consider your lectures. Are there central questions you can ask that could help to hold student interest? Where is the main action? Are there relevant, important, and engaging stories to tell?)

As the story of Oedipus unfolds, we see the major dramatic question evolving, often with each major complication, and reaching new levels of significance. Oedipus first sends for the blind prophet, Tiresias. Tiresias refuses to help, he and Oedipus quarrel, and Tiresias (in veiled prophetic language) accuses Oedipus himself of the murder. At this point, the major dramatic question changes: Is Oedipus indeed the killer he seeks? Who "sees" things more clearly, the sighted but hot-tempered king or the blind prophet? As the result of the accusation, Oedipus jumps to the conclusion that Tiresias and Creon are plotting to overthrow him and threatens to execute the traitors.

(If you open discussion about ethical issues in your discipline, for example, you can find similar "plot points" and questions. Explore these as a playwright might look for dramatic material. What will be engaging, potential grist for stimulating discussions?)

Sophocles creates a second major complication when Oedipus' wife Jocasta, attempting to smooth over the quarrel, tells Oedipus not to trust oracles. She points out that the oracle had warned Laius that he would be killed by his own son, but after the baby was put out on a mountain to die, Laius was murdered by robbers at a place where three roads meet. This revelation worries Oedipus; he suddenly remembers that he once killed an old man at a place where three roads meet. Oedipus sends for the only survivor of the attack, a shepherd who had reported that multiple robbers, not a single assassin, killed Laius. The major dramatic question has again evolved: Can oracles be trusted? Will Oedipus prove to be the murderer, even though that would contradict the oracle?

(Can you find key questions to raise in your lectures as you build toward conclusions?)

The third major complication in *Oedipus the King* arrives in the form of a messenger from Corinth, who informs Oedipus that his father, King Polybus, has died. Oedipus refuses to return to Corinth, however, citing an oracle warning him that he was destined to kill his father and marry his mother; since his mother is still alive, he won't risk fulfilling the second part of the prophecy. "No problem," the messenger replies. "She's not really your mother. You were adopted." The messenger reveals that he had been given the baby Oedipus by a Theban shepherd. With this complication, the major dramatic question shifts: Who is Oedipus? The simple detective story becomes a search for the nature of human identity.

(Telling more about the human stories in your discipline can add an element that may appeal to students on a more personal level. What were the twists and turns in the lives of the great thinkers, writers, activists? What lessons can students take from their lives?)

The Oedipus saga continues, as the shepherd arrives. (By one of those quirks of fate common in Greek tragedy, the shepherd who witnessed Laius' murder is the shepherd who gave the baby to the messenger). Under pressure, the shepherd finally admits that Oedipus is the son of Laius and Jocasta, his father's murderer and his mother's husband — Oedipus has unwittingly fulfilled the prophesy. This revelation (the major crisis) leads to another shift in the major dramatic question: What will Oedipus do now that he knows destiny does rule human life? What should be the response of any ethical human being to unbearable self-discovery?

(As you consider the current scene in your own discipline, can you find compelling stories of prophesy fulfilled? The stories are not always so dramatic. For example, what happens to those whose ideas get discredited when paradigms shift?)

Although Jocasta kills herself, Oedipus does not. He's certain now that his life has some purpose yet to be disclosed (major structural climax). He blinds himself, but he now possesses spiritual insight. He does not blame the gods for his downfall, but instead takes responsibility for his actions. The resolution of the play shows Oedipus going off into exile to follow where the gods will lead him.

(What happens to the "tragic figures" in your own discipline? How has history treated the greats? Again, life is generally less dramatic than Greek tragedies; although you may not find many "tragic figures," you're likely to be able to present some interesting characters in your field. For example, are there discoveries or creations that have been ignored, such as contributions by women or members of ethnic minority groups?)

Studying the structure of plays shows how playwrights use crises and complications to engage audience interest through stimulating questions. If you want to do more to sustain student interest throughout class, if you want to use lectures for more than transmission of knowledge, if you want to encourage your students to think more deeply about the significance of a topic, then you may want to use more of the human stories involved, with all their attendant questions and dilemmas.

You can, for instance, determine the major questions you want your students to consider and structure your lecture accordingly. Note how our analysis of Oedipus shows that the questions become increasingly more significant as the play progresses. All of the questions work on the simple level of suspense — What will happen? — and thus help sustain audience attention, but the questions also progressively involve the audience intellectually — What is the meaning of what is happening? When you teach, you can refer back to underlying concepts and objectives and thus help students better assimilate more of the central ideas and information.

In good drama, the emotions and the intellect work together. As audience members, we engage in the search for meaning after the playwright has drawn us into the story emotionally and we empathize with the characters; we can feel with Oedipus the horror of having to confront ourselves, to face the dreadful realization that we have done the very thing we most feared doing. Likewise, our lectures can do more to stimulate emotional identification as well as intellectual inquiry. As mentioned, you can relate the stories of great discoveries in your field or introduce relevant issues from the real world. Students will invest more energy in searching for answers to questions when they feel, on a personal level, that the material has meaning for them, that the questions raised are important.

Writers for the stage and screen learn to craft dialogue and actions that are central to a production's through-line. Everything, every little detail, has a purpose. These writers will also incorporate various elements to keep the audience engaged, in suspense, laughing, wondering, worrying, thinking. Writers will use surprises, plot twists, or conflicts to add drama and comedy. Similarly, they will focus on the timing of lines, actions and pacing, costuming, lighting, and choreography — all of which can contribute to the ability of individual audience members to engage their thoughts and feelings in the "willing suspension of disbelief."

Across an entire semester, you have only so much time to invest in any one lecture. However, if you explore a few new possibilities in depth, you may learn some things which can have lasting benefits. Consider the following:

- The next time you prepare lecture notes, consider leaving wide margins on both sides for additional notes, especially about delivery, including key questions.

- Step back and consider the entire lecture as a production, with an opening, a clear through-line, a pace that fits the audience and the material, and a *build* toward a conclusion or climax.

- Consider a practice run through the lecture/script. Call it a *rehearsal*, if only imagined.

- If possible, get someone to videotape your lecture and then analyze the "script" as you see it "performed." Look at it from the perspective of your students.

Exercises

1. Get a copy of a script from a library, a book store, a colleague, or a friend. Read it to get a better appreciation of the careful crafting involved.

2. Now rethink a recent lecture. Then plan one for the future. Investing some time in crafting one lecture may lead you to some valuable insights that generalize to others.

Hooking Students at the Start

A great deal of research supports the value of student engagement as an important factor in learning (e.g., Eble 1994; McKeachie 1994; Denham and Lieberman 1980). In his popular book on postsecondary teaching, Joseph Lowman (1995) insists that intellectual excitement (and the interest it generates) and rapport should be the two most important classroom concerns. Timpson and Bendel-Simso (1996) describe a number of concepts and choices that teachers in higher education have at their disposal for sustaining student interest; e.g., discovery and group learning, debates and discussions, demonstrations and role-plays, student-centered and problem-based learning.

While engagement is somewhat slippery to identify and measure as a researchable construct, students can certainly tell you whether or not they were absorbed in a particular lecture. They can describe what gets their attention, what sustains it, what allows them to drift off, and what turns them off completely. When asked to describe what has worked and what has not, teachers can also be remarkably accurate, identifying times when they felt that they were losing a class and what might have worked to get them back.

Plays and movies must have something that grabs the audience members in the first few minutes for a production to succeed. Without an effective *hook*, performances may feel long and audiences become restless. Interest must be piqued right away, curiosity whetted. Along with the story and action, lighting, costuming, and set combine to augment the impact of the hook. In class, the students' first impressions of a teacher can be important for the rest of the semester. Just as actors "make an entrance," so can you grab the attention of your students from your very first moment with them.

While viewers may disagree about the exact nature of the hook that worked for them, successful films grab their attention early. Whether in the animated version of *Peter Pan* or the Steven Spielberg remake of *Hook*, the kidnapping of the children by Captain Hook sets up the drama to follow. Most recently, Spielberg shrouds the opening to *Jurassic Park* in mystery as workers try to move a large container with something large, alive, and very ominous. Remember the accompanying soundtrack? Suddenly, one of the workers is pulled in and, by the sound of screams and chomps, killed and eaten. The hook for *Home Alone* comes when the parents drive to the airport, board their flight, and take off before realizing that they've forgotten their son. The hook for *Big* occurs when the Tom Hanks character wakes up the morning after his interaction with a strange mechanical genie and discovers that his wish to be big has been granted. The hook for *ET* happens when the aliens leave hastily when pressed by a menacing human search party and leave behind one of their own. The darkness of that opening night scene, with all the headlights and flashlights, the urgency in the voices, the foreboding soundtrack, the low shots and quick cuts — all combine to create a sense of impending danger. *Gone With The Wind* pulls us in from the very beginning, when the roguish Rhett Butler shows a riveting interest in the flighty Scarlett

O'Hara amid all the brash talk about a "quick victory for the noble South."

For teaching, Hunter (1982) describes this hook as *set*, those comments or actions, activities or experiences that pull students into the lesson for that day, that help to engage their emotions and focus their minds. (This use of the word "set" should not be confused with the "set" used for stage and film.) Students enter your classroom from various other realities — prior classes, home, friends, studies, eating, playing, napping, working, or perhaps just hanging out. Your lecture, like the theatrical production, should capture everyone's interest early on.

Jim Boyd (Philosophy, Colorado State University) often has music playing when his Eastern religions class begins. That's a wonderful way to pull students into the material, to give them a gentle reminder about the sanctity of the classroom space, to let them know that class time has begun (Boyd will start the music five to ten minutes before class officially begins), and to encourage them to reflect, even meditate. Note his attempt to a more holistic approach to learning, since meditation is so central to many Eastern religious practices. Boyd will also refer to the music during class as a concrete example of a particular religious or cultural practice.

What can work as a hook in a lecture?

- A good question can challenge students to think or alert them to connections with events in the news.

- Something puzzling or complex can stimulate creative alternatives.

- A demonstration at the very outset can raise questions and illustrate principles that you can discuss later.

- A brief activity that puts students together to work on a question or a problem can energize everyone from the very beginning of class.

- Some description of the personalities or human drama that are in the background can help personalize the course and sustain student interest.

The key is to have the idea of the hook in mind, to be willing to experiment, to look for that early engagement, and to assess the impact of what you try.

Exercises

1. Try to identify the hook the next time you watch a movie or television drama. Note your level of engagement. The movie industry knows how important the hook is and will also add a few carefully edited and fast-paced previews of coming attractions. These advertisements then serve as mini-hooks. In the last several television seasons, producers have been starting their shows with action, not the traditional theme and credits, to engage viewers before they even identify the show. By doing this they are challenging what has been a nearly sacred tradition of a long commercial break between shows, in the hope of grabbing viewers — lest they start channel-surfing or consider doing something else — and making the most of a strong lead-in to the next show; i.e., its hook.

2. Now watch another film or play and pay particular attention to the entrances made by the actors. A key here is to *detach* yourself from the story line and focus solely on the entrances. This kind of *distance* can be important in learning how to identify *objectively* the elements of effective presentations.

3. Think about lectures that had good hooks. Try to develop a hook for an upcoming talk.

The Classroom as a Set

Many teachers in higher education tend to ignore their instructional spaces. Sure, most have preferences for certain rooms and know about terrible rooms that are too cold or too hot or have bad acoustics. In too many classrooms, both old and refurbished, the desks are bolted, making small group assignments nearly impossible. You undoubtedly have your own horror stories about equipment that failed at the worst time, about rooms that proved to be too small or too big, about light streaming in through windows and making it hard to see overheads or slides. However, most of us just carry on as best we can, believing that it's the subject, the information, the ideas that really matter.

You probably doubt that you can do much with your assigned rooms anyway. For example, you may ignore whatever bulletin boards are available, leaving them for students and advertisers to cover. Even if you wanted to take the bulletin board more seriously, what would you do?

The lesson from the stage here is that the set is integral to the success of a production, so much so that the set designer is given billing near equal to that of the director and reports to the producer. For example, every script provides scenic directions, although writers differ in the amount of detail they provide. The set designer works closely with the director to provide the desired backdrop for the production within the space available and the limitations of resources and budget.

But just what can you do within the limitations of the "classroom stage" to which you are assigned? What lessons can we learn from the theatre? Consider the following ... .

Think of the overhead or the board as having more creative possibilities. One prof in a large class invites students to put relevant announcements on the board before class to save time; this makes for a fun backdrop with lots of interesting reading. Some teachers put the day's goals or activities up as a visual reference to help keep everyone focused. Showing a videotape or film can transform your lecture hall into a movie theatre. Music or other sounds can also help engage students. Posters can add color, visuals, and inspiring thoughts. You can also change the position of the podium and thereby your relationship to your students.

In a smaller classroom, you could move the chairs and tables into different configurations. You could include demonstrations of various kinds. You could organize a field trip, as a sort of set change. You could use other rooms on occasion, perhaps to take advantage of laboratory equipment or to better accommodate small group activities. When telling an anecdote or providing an example, you can use careful descriptions to evoke the imaginations of your students and help set an imaginary stage. Once you reconceptualize your class as a set, you may find a new world of ideas to enhance the learning environment.

George Wallace (Natural Resource Management, Colorado State University) has a real gift for conceptualizing his teaching "stage" in a very big way, one that often goes far beyond his classroom walls or the campus itself. In a course on multicultural education, for example, Wallace would often have students go on a *neighborhood walk* through a local barrio, talk to area residents, and get a personal feel for the people and places they were reading about. For one course on environmental impact, he has a long and detailed field assignment that requires students to explore a number of local sites. These experiences also supplement readings and help form the basis for a very rich discussion in class.

Exercises

1. Recall a lecture that you attended for which the room was used in ways that added to the impact of the message. Make a note of what worked for you and why.

2. Now rethink one of your lectures for which you could have done more with the classroom set. What can you do in the future to explore this potential?

The Roles You Play

As a lecturer you do much more than lecture. You may have to play several roles. Of course, you must be expert in your own discipline as well as a skilled presenter. But you can also help yourself by also playing director, producer, set designer, choreographer, customer, props manager, and even roadie — someone has to haul all those papers and props around! Over the years, if you have become highly specialized, you may also need to sustain a more general command of the field so you can teach introductory and lower-level classes.

Let's look more closely at these roles. Before class begins, you work as producer, organizing everything from text selection to the placement of readings on reserve at the library, from preparation of the course syllabus to the scheduling of guest speakers. Once class begins, you become responsible for a wide range of activities, from clarifying class procedures to ensuring the effective use of overheads, slides, videotapes, and film. As a lecturer, you function as master of ceremonies, reminding the students about earlier material, announcing upcoming events, introducing the day's topics, fielding questions that arise, moderating discussions, handling unexpected interruptions, adding final comments at the very end, and so forth.

Once class begins, you also serve as your own warm-up act, getting students engaged and helping them to focus on the material at hand. As a facilitator of learning, you invariably juggle a mixture of carrots and sticks. As judge and jury for each course, you decide upon the final grade. As mediator, you may have to resolve conflicts that arise, from complaints about grades to squabbles within student project groups. As a surrogate parent, you may be asked about any number of nonacademic issues as well.

So what can we offer you from the stage that might help you manage this degree of role complexity? First, we encourage you to become more aware of these roles. Playwrights take great care in developing each character. Producers make sure that everything is organized ahead of time. Directors ensure that the actual performance holds together. Your ability to run through these performance roles before teaching can give you a very helpful systematic check.

A concrete example might help here. Michael Lipe (Music, Theatre, and Dance, Colorado State University) is a colleague blessed with a wonderful tenor voice. He often takes leading roles in performances on and off campus. Relatively short and heavy, he would not seem the likely choice to play a romantic lead. Yet in one memorable opera production of Carmen, he found himself playing opposite a soprano, his love interest, who was physically stunning, taller than him, and quite thin. While their voices blended beautifully, their differences in size and shape made them initially incongruous as a couple, almost unbelievable for some in the audience. Yet Lipe exuded such confidence in his role that he quickly won over audiences. His resonant voice and skill as an actor seemed to make the physical differences disappear.

In like manner, you can study the various roles required of you and learn how to develop each as needed. As the master of ceremonies, you need to engage your students. As public speaker, you need to project to the last row and enunciate clearly. As an expert, you need to be knowledgeable and prepared. As an enthusiast of your discipline, you need to find ways to share your enthusiasm with your students. As a human being, you need to care about your students, to show sensitivity for them as fellow human beings, to make better use of their diverse backgrounds and personalities and experiences and interests, to challenge them to make the most of themselves and of the opportunities around them, to help them deal with others with empathy and resolve conflicts in constructive and caring ways, to organize activities that require them to work cooperatively, to inspire them to question, analyze, synthesize, and evaluate.

Loren Crabtree (History, Colorado State University) is a wonderful teacher who successfully mixes his expertise as an Asian scholar with a studied commitment to student learning and a caring climate in class. Although stretched to fulfill his responsibilities as dean of liberal arts, he wanted to try a series of instructional innovations one semester. (The best teachers seem ever open to new possibilities.) To his more conventional approach of assigned readings and lecture/discussion, he added a course requirement of a cooperative presentation. What was new to his role as teacher was the supervision and guidance required to make these projects successful, including intervening when one group got derailed, when a member of another was repeatedly absent, and when another group never really rose to the challenge to do more than divide the time available among the group members and present mini-lectures!

The playwright integrates all the various characters and actions in a careful mosaic that is believable, at least on paper. The director makes sure that it all works on stage. In many ways, as a lecturer you do the same. Each role should be "believable" (effective), both in theory and practice, and they should all be tied together by the through-line (course goals and objectives). With awareness and practice you can fit all the things that you do in your course together into a mosaic. For example, the exams you write can match the objectives you state in your syllabus or in class, your enthusiasm for the subject can be reflected in the energy you bring to class and your interest in starting on time, and your concern for your students can show in your willingness to listen to their ideas and their concerns.

Exercises

1. Think about an actor who is credited with a wide range of roles. Dustin Hoffman and Meryl Streep come to mind for us. Both actors have the reputation of working very hard at every new role. It was widely reported that Hoffman spent a great deal of time learning about his character for the *Rain Man*, for example, and Streep did many of her own stunts in *Wild River*. Study, experimentation, experience, and practice are the keys here. Think about the various hats you must wear as a lecturer. Which are most comfortable? Which are

not? Keep a journal as you observe yourself for several class periods. Try to consciously become more of the characters you need to be for your class to be most successful.

2. Note that some actors have been trapped by a certain kind of role and now they seem typecast. Can Sylvester Stallone effectively do more than Rocky-like films? Could Marilyn Monroe have been more than a "sex goddess"? Have you been trapped into certain characterizations that limit your use of the lecture? For example, as an expert, are you uncomfortable with small group assignments where it seems that the "blind are leading the blind"? At times, your role as "expert" may keep your students from learning more independently.

The Roles You Could Play

As a lecturer, you bring your training, knowledge, and experiences into your classes. As we have already suggested, why not bring along more of the personalities behind some of that knowledge, the stories that form the backdrop of your field? For example, science texts tend to describe facts and theories in a very straightforward manner with little discussion of the humans who brought each discovery to light. Why not share more of the thinking and creativity, the frustrations and perseverance, that underlie these discoveries? How did the greats overcome the ignorance of their times, the prevailing paradigms about truth, and strike out in new directions? For example, how did Galileo overcome the "facts" that were taught to him as well as the prohibitions of the church to reconceptualize the relationship of the earth to the sun?

Surely your students ought to know as much about the process of discovery, the thinking and creativity required, as you expect them to know about the discoveries themselves, the *products* of research. It certainly seems that the future will require more creativity, more skill with problem-solving and group dynamics, greater abilities to work as team members. What is your role in preparing future generations? Can your undergraduates participate more in research? How should the curriculum change to accommodate all this?

Role-playing can *dramatically* enrich any lecture. Imagine the impact of introducing a whole range of characters into a lecture about the "discovery" of the Americas in 1492, for example. What was the perspective of Native Americans, of the soldiers who accompanied

Columbus, of the royalty in Spain who bankrolled the exploration, of the missionaries who accompanied later explorations? "Discoveries" like this are found in all disciplines and the people involved have great dramatic potential for engaging our students in the facts and theories that they study.

What advantages might there be in researching such characters before playing their roles? First, you can delve into the actual process of discovery and share with students the actions, motivations, and relationships in these stories, which can serve as examples of thinking and creativity. Second, you can broaden and deepen your own understanding of a field. Third, such efforts can breathe new life into old subjects and reinvigorate your interest.

The value of role-playing may be especially high at this point in history, as we find the canon in literature challenged, as we rethink expert opinion and presumed objectivity, as we analyze the contextual background of writers and their environments, as we examine the growing importance of the sciences and the decline of the arts. The flexibility and empathy acquired from assuming a variety of roles may prove helpful when we seek more diversity in interpretation, when we ask students to think for themselves and participate more in the *construction* of meaning.

Burgoyne has used role-playing in theatre history classes, courses that in theatre departments are normally considered "academic" rather than "performance" classes. In American Theatre History, students researched their assigned subjects, then presented oral reports to their classmates — in the character of a significant historical American actor, director, or designer from the period studied. The student presenters wore appropriate costume pieces and brought in relevant photographs, recordings, etc. Following each report, the presenter remained in character to respond to questions from classmates. In World Theatre History II, each student reported on a major theorist of the modern theatre (Stanislavski, Brecht, Artaud, etc.). Following the reports, all the students participated in a mock debate — each in the role of his or her theorist. Burgoyne found that significant issues about the nature of acting and the role of theatre in society came to life for the students, as each ardently argued his or her theorist's point of view.

Timpson also makes regular use of spontaneous role-playing to illustrate certain points, especially when skills are involved and a lecture or discussion can only accomplish so much. At these points, students need to see certain techniques modeled and then have some practice with them. For example, during a presentation on effective communications — reflective listening, I-messages, and consensus — one student described a situation where he as tutor was constantly in demand to help students in his study session solve this or that problem, even when they had just been over certain material, sometimes two and three times. What follows are the alternative responses that Timpson offered and role-played on the spot, responses that showed how the tutor could emphasize that students should think through more systematically their struggles with learning before running for help:

- "It seems that you're having difficulty with that problem. Can you say why?"

- "When we review material and then students come running to me for help right away, I get frustrated because no learning seems to be occurring. Can we discuss this further?"

- "When so many students need help after going through similar solutions, I think we need a new plan in this class. Let's use the consensus model to develop something we can all agree to for guiding our study sessions here."

Timpson's experiences in theatre workshops and productions have pushed him to use more spontaneous role-playing as a way to augment more traditional but limited verbal analyses.

Exercises

1. Reflect on the greats in your own field, those who have influenced your own thinking. Consider coming to class as one of these characters or enlisting the help of someone else to do that. Let your students interact as if this person were actually there.

2. Consider the variety of roles you could add through student presentations. Although you may feel inhibited about "acting in public," there are people in every class and on every campus who enjoy this kind of challenge and who can handle it well. Or contact a colleague who works with actors, on campus or in the community, and recruit some to play roles. What fun you can have when you open your classes to these sources of creativity and energy!

Techniques to Enhance Your Roles

It's one thing to recommend a variety of roles, but something very different to help teachers develop and refine them. Here, lessons from the stage may be especially helpful.

Actors use a variety of approaches to get into their stage roles. One set of techniques permits them to work from the *inside-out* and draw on their own experiences and feelings for the emotional foundation of their roles. Another technique permits them to work from the *outside-in* and adopt the physical mannerisms, actions, gestures, movements, and facial expressions required for their roles.

Inside-Out

Perhaps the best-known "inside-out" technique is "affective memory" — when actors draw upon their past experiences to recreate particular feelings. It can be very difficult to be sad on cue, for example, night after night. Consequently, some performers will "relive" certain events that produced similar feelings in their own lives, using meditation and concentration to recall as much detail as possible. Once those feelings arise again, these actors can then transfer them to the stage. You may want to try this approach when you need to get up for teaching, when you want to show your enthusiasm, when you need to crank up your energy level to project effectively in a large lecture hall, when the routine of work bores you or the critical comments from a few students depress you.

We all have had good days and bad, some great classes and some that we would rather forget. We're naturally more enthusiastic about some topics and a bit bored with others. Some classes may feel very special, with just the right chemistry; for these we feel more focused, clear, responsive, and effective. However, for some classes, we may need to contend with lethargy, inattention, or such disturbances as late arrivals, chatter, and early departures. This effective "inside-out" approach may help us draw on the emotions and experiences that have accompanied our best teaching in the past, to help us ride through difficult periods and teach more effectively in the present.

Burgoyne warns, however, that affective memory techniques can be problematic with actors, dredging up past personal traumas and opening a psychological Pandora's Box. She has moved away from that sort of invasive technique for actor training, though she fully recognizes that many actors use it. If you use an affective memory approach, Burgoyne suggests that you focus on the sensory impressions associated with the memory and not on the emotions themselves.

Outside-In

Another technique that actors routinely use requires analysis from a more behavioral perspective. The actor breaks the role down into a series of actions, poses, gestures, facial expressions, movements, and so on. Very analytically, the actor will create the "look" he or she wants for a particular character, one that will make sense to the audience. They do not access inner feelings, as with affective memory techniques; they work just with appearances and actions — what is observable.

In teaching, consider an important quality like "enthusiasm." You can describe it — you create the appropriate gestures, movements, expressions, vocal pitch, and timing. You can likewise describe the behaviors for other qualities that you need in your classroom roles: e.g., the patience to listen well when students raise questions or to wait for them to formulate their responses, the agility to facilitate debates and discussions within the lecture format, the concentration to sustain a focus on a lesson's through-line (learning objectives). How fast should you make your movements? Your speech? What about pitch? What gestures would help?

Exercises

1. Think about one of your best lectures. Visualize yourself back in that class: feel the room, your students, yourself. What do you look like? How are you moving? How do you sound? What are you feeling as you teach? Now, can you use those feelings in the present, to energize your preparation for an upcoming lecture? Can you recycle now some of what worked then?

2. Try both approaches — emotional recall and technical analysis. Which works better for you? Would a mixture of the two be even more effective? Your goal in using either or both of these techniques should be to teach more effectively in a *natural* way. Work on finding an appropriate *comfort level* with these approaches.

Pacing

Any good script incorporates a variety of actions and feelings. An audience can only absorb so much tragedy or banter or suspense during any one stretch. Playwrights change the mood or pace to augment, contrast, or shade certain emotions. Actions on stage can build toward a climax in overt or subtle ways.

Similarly, every good lecture works at a certain pace — not so fast as to leave students feeling overwhelmed and weary from taking notes, not so slow that they drift off. Although you may have a firm grasp of your subject, your students will not: they can suffer from "information overload." Also, especially in large introductory courses, some students will not share your own enthusiasm for the material, while others may be downright hostile, for any number of reasons. Yet even the best and the most enthusiastic students have limited attention spans.

All students can benefit if you put more variety into your lectures. That variety could be organizational: after an introductory *preview*, you might periodically break up your lecture (information transmission) with reminders about underlying core concepts, to help your students with the intellectual organization of all that they have to assimilate. (Ausubel's (1963) groundbreaking research on the *advance organizer* demonstrates the importance of a conceptual framework for supporting student learning and retention.) You could add variety to your lectures in smaller ways; for example, you might sprinkle examples and demonstrations throughout, to provide concrete references to the real world and a counterweight to more abstract and conceptual teachings, or raise questions to sharpen the focus. Then, in your conclusion, you could recap the lecture, reemphasize the essential points, remind your students of the examples, and/or return to your questions.

Variety in pacing may make a world of difference to students who are struggling. One incident really brought this point home to Timpson.

One day in class, he called on M, one of his best students, to respond to what another had said. "I can't answer that," she said. A bit perturbed, thinking she wasn't listening, Timpson quickly called on another student. The next morning he found a rather angry email message from M noting that she had not heard what had been said and wanted it repeated. She went on to complain about the fast pace of class, which made discussions brief and superficial, she thought.

Timpson apologized for cutting her off and admitted that the large size of the class (75 students) made him anxious whenever the pace slowed.

In class a few days later, M asked for more information about an assignment concerning computer applications. When no one else admitted to sharing that same concern, Timpson first decided to discuss this concern with M after class. However, he then thought to slow down and ask for students familiar with the Internet to come up to the front and describe their progress with that assignment. Five came forward and the resulting discussion was very productive for everyone; it turned out that a lot of students were unsure about the assignment, but unwilling to admit it. Timpson lost 20 minutes from his plan for that day, but those 20 minutes proved well worth the shift in plans and change of pace.

As is true in the theatre, even the best material can suffer from a dry and monotonous exposition. Consider putting that material onto paper and using more of your class time for the kinds of interactions that take greater advantage of the talents in the room. Share your energy and enthusiasm: it can make all the difference in engaging your students. For example, Irene Vernon (English, Colorado State University) teaches a tough course on the law surrounding U.S. relationships with Native Americans — wars, treaties, broken promises, and governmental deception. The material is difficult because all that tortured history is encased within complex legal documents and court opinions, primary sources that are further complicated by differences in language and custom. Recognizing the difficulty in the material, Vernon effectively mixes her big personality and her booming voice with a varied pace and structure which shifts from lecture to small group work to general discussion and back again.

Exercises

1. Track the pacing of a favorite movie or play. Note the periods of comic relief. A great thriller is usually more like a roller coaster than a nonstop reign of terror: periods of calm and unpredictability heighten the fear factor. In the classroom, many teachers use regular reminders about what will be on an upcoming exam to jolt students into paying closer attention. While you should minimize the use of fear in class, there are other possibilities worth exploring — your use of pauses

and silences, discussions or debates, free-writing exercises to promote student reflection.

2. Examine one of your recent lectures for pacing. Could you have varied the pace more to heighten engagement?

3. Rethink the pacing of an upcoming lecture. Are there periods of relief from the usual routine, from the presentation of information or completion of problem sets? Could regular stops for a few questions or comments give you a chance to emphasize certain key points? Could these stops also allow students some relief from the intensity of taking notes to actually think about the ideas and issues?

Warming Up

This is a bit of a repeat, but the lecture format can be a very pressured situation, especially as class size increases, and we know that you will benefit from some warm-up. Nothing in teaching comes closer to a stage performance than a lecture. Warm-ups are vital to most performers, who often begin their rehearsal and pre-performance time together with stretches, vocal exercises, and the like. Being prepared emotionally and physically for class can add much to your intellectual preparation of the content.

As we have often repeated, your energy and enthusiasm mean a lot to students. The more alert you are, the better you can see their struggles and the more sensitively you can respond. A warm-up that includes a review of student names can help you make your interactions with them more personal and improve your classroom climate. For a description of exercise suggestions, reread the chapter on warming up.

Movements

Few lectures require much in the way of movement. Routinely, you enter the class and lay out your materials at the front. You may use the board, an overhead, a film, a video, or slides to illustrate key points or examples. You may wander a bit at the front of the class. Rarely do you have anything "staged," "blocked," or "choreographed." If you move much at all, you may just pace as you think and talk. Is this effective for you? What else might be possible?

Some teachers have abandoned the traditional lecture approach as too limiting of interactions and involvement. Using a case study approach allows Marty Fettman (Pathology, Colorado State University) to facilitate discussions with classes of 100, 200, or more. He may move around the lecture hall as students offer their ideas and others take issue. In this way, his students analyze the presenting symptoms and discuss possible remedies. The cases are true to life and force students to act like practicing veterinarians. As Fettman moves out from behind the lectern, he physically shifts the focus from conveying his expertise to a large-group, guided-discovery process. He really challenges students to think for themselves. His energy, movements, and creativity add life to a professional curriculum often dominated by lecture-based information-giving. Fettman seems to thoroughly enjoy the challenge of this kind of dynamic and interactive teaching.

Using small-group assignments or student presentations would permit you to get students up, moving, and participating. Apart from the obvious benefits of variety in helping to sustain student interest, opportunities for more active learning can dramatically improve student understanding. Developmentalists like Piaget (1952), Bruner (1966), Kohlberg (1981), Gilligan (1982), and Perry (1981) have long emphasized the power of activity in promoting deeper learning. A new generation of developmentalists, including Tharp and Gallimore (1988) and Rogoff (1990), continue to reaffirm the relationship between active learning and the development of critical thinking skills.

Perhaps just as important, new critics of the traditional information-driven and expert-dominated lecture (e.g., Belenky et al. 1986; Tobias, 1990) are also calling for more participatory learning in higher education, so that women and minority students in particular can get more of the peer support and assistance they often desire. Active and cooperative learning within a social context becomes important to many for success in large classes in which teachers feel the need to cover a great deal of material.

Historically, the more traditional approach to course design and grading has often served a gatekeeping function, encouraging an impersonal and competitive environment in classes where norm-referenced assessment (grading on the curve) have defined class climate and discouraged cooperation. When teachers try to sift through these masses of students to uncover "those few with potential," they inevitably — surprise, surprise! — find students much like themselves.

A massive cloning process results, one that tends to replicate the values, perspectives, styles, gender, and culture of those teaching, most often older white males. When this occurs, everyone suffers: some students get "weeded" out for the wrong reasons, the disciplines lose out on a rich and diverse talent base, and the pursuit of new knowledge is compromised, as the cloning process does more to sustain prevailing paradigms than to support healthy and creative challenges.

We think that lessons from the stage can help teachers become more aware of the "choreography" that occurs in their classes and what may enhance learning. Every script written for production will have directions for stage movements, who should be where for which lines and actions and when. Although much is left to the talents of actors, directors, and choreographers to discover — how best to "block out" the action and physicalize what is only on paper — writers sketch out basic movements in the script. Unless improvisation is called for — which is quite rare — no one wants any surprises on stage.

While spontaneous digressions, questions, and discussions can stimulate learning and challenge students to think, teachers who use the planned lecture can also benefit from notations about movements or blocking. For example:

- You could write yourself reminders to get out from behind the lectern when you think you are reading too much from prepared notes and losing the attention of your students.

- You could remind yourself to move toward a student who asks a question and get that student's name, to help personalize the class more.

- After giving a small-group assignment, you could also make a note to yourself to move quickly around the room and help keep students on task.

- You could indicate when you would want to use the overhead projector or where you could stand when slides are showing so as not to block any views.

In *The Teacher Moves: An Analysis of Nonverbal Activity*, Grant and Hennings (1971) reported on a variety of studies that affirm the importance of teacher movement in the classroom. In one study, teachers were videotaped and their movements analyzed. Surprising to many, a full 80% of these movements were deemed relevant to the instructional process, although not in ways you might expect: over 60% involved *conducting* behavior (controlling participation or obtaining attention), about 30% involved *wielding* (moving toward action, picking up assignments, reading), but less than 10% involved *acting* (emphasizing, illustrating, pantomiming, role-playing, etc.).

Grant and Hennings offered several recommendations for teachers:

- *Eliminate contradictory cues.* Too many teachers undercut what they think is exciting when they deliver their lectures in a dry and rigid manner. Students will believe what they hear and *see.* Allow yourself to get animated when appropriate, or reflective when important questions arise, or even confused when a problem gets complex.

- *Increase the right kind of nonverbal cues.* Teachers dominate much of the allotted classroom time, and nearly all of the time in lectures. Look for opportunities to substitute nonverbal cues for verbal expressions. For example, you can reflect pleasure over a particular response in a facial expression or a hand gesture and allow more space for other students to participate.

- *Eliminate irrelevant nonverbal cues.* Given that 20% of the teacher's classroom movements were found to be personal and unrelated to instruction, you can try to minimize irrelevant and nonverbal cues. If the statistics are not enough to convince you, just think back to your own teachers who were plagued by distracting nervous mannerisms — playing with their hair or beard, constantly adjusting their glasses, blinking excessively, jingling keys or coins and so on.

Stage directors know that movement draws attention, so they carefully choreograph all on-stage movement. The movement may look spontaneous, but it has been thoroughly outlined and rehearsed. In class you may not want to plan your gestures, but some basic stage principles about how to use movement for emphasis can prove helpful.

Actors and directors use movement to "point" (emphasize) significant lines. The principles of pointing involve the relationship between movement and speech. There are four possible ways for an actor to move with a line of dialogue: 1) before the line; 2) after the line; 3) during the line; 4) after part of the line and before the rest of the line.

To illustrate how pointing works, consider the line "Gwendolyn, will you marry me?" from Oscar Wilde's *The Importance of Being Earnest.* Let's say that the movement the actor will perform is to kneel to

Gwendolyn. He can 1) kneel first, then say the line; 2) say the line, then kneel; 3) say the line while kneeling; 4) say part of the line, for instance, "Gwendolyn, will you ..." then kneel and finish the line, "marry me?" Try performing the line all four ways. Note that: 1) moving before the line emphasizes the line; 2) moving after the line emphasizes the movement; 3) moving during the line de-emphasizes both the line and the movement; 4) movement that breaks up a line emphasizes the part of the line that follows the movement.

The application of these principles to lecturing is subtle but real: the best place for you to move in relationship to a climactic, significant statement is probably just before the statement — or the most important words in that statement — to draw attention to it. The movement can be as obvious as pounding on the table or as subtle as a step, a gesture, or a turn — or even nothing at all: if you have been pacing, a sudden stop can be quite dramatic.

The principles of pointing also make it clear that you should not move during the significant statement; such movement will distract the audience and downplay your important point. Good comics instinctively understand timing and pointing — you won't see one move during the punch line of a joke!

Exercises

1. To become more aware, you may need new forms of feedback. Have someone — a friend, colleague, or student — come in to track your movements during class, noting what happens, when, and where. What effects do your movements appear to have on student engagement (listening, attentiveness)? Or have one of your lectures videotaped and get a good look at yourself in action. These observations alone may suggest areas for improvement. Discussing them with others can get you valuable additional insights. (Videotaping your class may seem intimidating, but once you get past the initial "shock" of your own appearance — like many professionals, you are probably your own worst critic — this *purely objective* viewpoint can prove very helpful. It will also give you a good sense of what your students see.) Using both sources of feedback in concert may be ideal.

2. Keep a journal in which you jot down your impressions, worries, hopes, etc., before class and then again immediately after class.

Review your thoughts and reactions to earlier classes. What patterns emerge?

3. Once you decide to make a change, either to eliminate movements that are distracting or to add some to enhance your lecture, give yourself several trials. Habits are difficult to break and new ones as difficult to implant. Experiment with movement, using reminders in your notes.

4. Some teachers move too much — pacing nervously across the front of the room, or continuing to talk while moving toward the chalkboard, which may make some words inaudible. Here again, you can learn a lesson from the stage. Actors have learned that it is easier to do something than to try *not* to do something. For instance, if an actor has fidgety hands, the director will often give him or her something specific to do with them — a character gesture or a stage property to work with. If you discover that you have a nervous habit to break, look for a specific action that you can substitute for the nervous habit. If you have a tendency to pace aimlessly, find a way of grounding yourself, perhaps through centering. (Try the centering exercise in our chapter on performance-enhancing exercises.) While you're learning the new habit, you can write into your lecture script periodic cues to remind yourself of the desired behavior.

Voice

Few teachers know much about the physiology of the voice or the nuances of speech that can greatly affect their teaching. Teachers can learn a lot from performers, who have long known about the benefits of appropriate pauses and timing, of projection and volume, of pitch and inflection, of good articulation and clear enunciation.

Most people judge others in part on their speech. What do your students think of you from your speech patterns? We cannot expect to do justice to each of these areas here, but we hope to provide enough of an explanation to raise your awareness and get you started.

As we noted earlier, a pause can serve a variety of functions in the theatre: to underscore the conflict of a scene, to hold for a laugh, and most often to allow the audience to wonder, "What will happen next?" A pause can be used in class for similar purposes. Even without any background as a performer, you can recognize the benefits when time for reflection helps deepen learning.

Timing is everything, it has been said. Those of us who have heard a superb lecturer or watched a great actor have admired their sense of timing. Understanding how rapidly or slowly to deliver a particular line or how long to hold a pause can help actors make their performances more powerful. The same ability can help you engage your students and add variety, surprise, and life to your presentation.

However important pauses and timing may be, they mean little without projection and volume, pitch and inflection, articulation and enunciation.

Your students must be able to hear your voice clearly, even in the very back of a large lecture hall. Use any amplification available, to reach your students and to spare your voice. Again, we recommend warm-up exercises.

Public speakers find that two of the most difficult aspects of voice are *pitch* and *inflection*. Pitch is the quality of vocal sound, the relative highs and lows (i.e., number of vibrations per second), while inflection represents the rise and fall of the voice. A third aspect, *intonation*, is a matter of the particular tones. The three are essential to making our words come alive.

We all appreciate teachers and performers who can add feeling and nuances to their words. In poetic drama, such as Shakespeare, the actor's vocal work can be as varied and melodic as that of a singer. In melodrama and farce, we may accept exaggerated vocal expression — a squeal of embarrassment or a gasp of shock — because of the unrealistic style of the play. In realistic drama, which reflects our daily lives, we expect actors to give the illusion of speaking naturally and spontaneously.

Students expect their teachers to speak naturally, but lecturers, like actors, can benefit from vocal training to make their voices more expressive. While you may find limited need for using the full range of your voice, changes in volume, pitch, and inflection can help you sustain student attention and communicate more effectively. Consider the following:

- Vary your volume, pitch, and inflection. A monotone rings a death knell for any presentation! Seek out a colleague whom you trust and ask him or her to attend one of your classes and assess your monotonal tendencies.

- Punctuate key points by increasing your volume.

- Explore the use of near whispers to express sadness and sensitivity.

- Speed up your talk to reflect your enthusiasm.

- When you read a passage from a previous era, perhaps out of the history of your discipline, try to capture the right tone.

Anyone who communicates with an audience — whether from the stage or in class — also needs clear articulation and enunciation. This may be a concern particularly for teachers who have a regional dialect, who learned English as a second language, or who have a speaking disability; for these people we would recommend consulting with a speech expert on campus. However, many of us are just lazy in our speech; that may be fine in casual conversations, but we might need to work on our articulation and enunciation for the classroom.

Exercises

1. Experiment with a variety of warm-ups before class, from humming a favorite melody to running up and down your vocal range with *la la la la*. You may never have had any formal training or practice, but you can still benefit from some vocal exercises. If nothing else, they can make you more aware about inflection, pitch, and intonation.

2. Record yourself on audiotape to hear how you sound in class. Then try a videotape to see how well your voice matches what you are doing with your facial expressions, gestures, movements, props, etc.

Note: More extensive vocal exercises appear in the section on warm-ups.

Props

Undoubtedly, you make extensive use of "props" (short for "stage properties"), but you just don't think of them that way. Anything that you use to augment what you say can be considered a prop, including the lectern, chalk, the overhead, slides, videotapes, films, materials for demonstrations, a table, a chair — anything. You could even include the intellectual "things" you use to augment instruction —

cases for law or business, problems for medical and health science study, word and story problems in mathematics. While every teacher makes some use of props, anyone could improve with exposure to new ideas, a willingness to experiment and to receive feedback, and a desire to improve through practice.

Do you need props for every lecture to be effective? Not necessarily. Do you remember Professor Kingsley (John Houseman) in the film and TV show *Paper Chase*? He rarely used props — only his experience, authority, and commanding presence. In *Dead Poets Society*, English teacher John Keating (Robin Williams) used a range of facial expressions, vocal inflections, volume, accents, body movements, postures, and gestures.

However, everyone can benefit from thinking about props more consciously. Let us share an example from one of our classes ....

Piaget has categorized cognitive development into distinct stages through which young people move as they mature. He has also identified certain tasks that serve to mark movement into more advanced stages.

When Timpson lectures about one of these tasks — the conservation of length — his students often struggle to understand that children can think in *qualitatively* different terms. Before age six, it is common for a child to say that a pipe cleaner has gotten shorter when it is bent in the middle. If you override your own logical thought processes, you can clearly "see" (literally) that the end points are closer together. The young child concludes that the pipe cleaner has gotten shorter.

In time, children are able to override this visual domination with a more logical conclusion: because nothing was taken away, the pipe cleaner must still be the same length as before. Using a pipe cleaner in class as a prop has helped Timpson demonstrate this phenomenon. Showing a videotape of first-graders struggling with this concept of conservation, some insisting that the pipe cleaner is indeed shorter, then provides the conclusive visual evidence that his students need. Learning about all this through lectures or reading alone is just not as effective.

Lots of other examples come to mind. A physicist brings in a pendulum to demonstrate properties and problems, to supplement words with actions. A sociologist brings in large portraits and photographs of the writers he covers in his survey class; seeing these faces seems to help some students relate better to each writer, to visually set each within a historical context. A lecturer in music will use a piano to illustrate various concepts; having the piano available allows him to be more flexible, which is especially valuable when students raise questions, and to simply share the joy of music. In all three case, the props also seem to permit the teachers to digress a bit and add more personal and engaging information to theoretical material.

What is working here is profoundly important to teaching and learning. We know from so many different sources now that there are distinct advantages in appealing to all the senses. Students have different sensory strengths and preferences, different learning styles. Using visuals or participatory demonstrations pushes students to engage more than their listening and note-taking skills. Multi-sensory input can strengthen memory, providing more cues for recall. Active learning can energize everyone.

In class, props can also include the most common of items. For example, a text can become a prop when the teacher holds it up while making summary comments. John Finley, a classics professor at Harvard, was famous for roaming the stage at Sanders Theatre while holding the microphone chord as it trailed behind him, periodically making rather grandiose flips of the chord when he had to change direction. These simple theatrics helped enliven his lectures about Greek and Roman drama. Every campus has its own stories; we could all cite examples of props that worked famously — and some that bombed.

On stage, the use of any prop is very carefully assessed and orchestrated in terms of a particular scene, action, or character. Playwrights, directors, set designers, and performers know full well the importance of using props for a specific purpose. The same can be true in class. If you do not use any props at all, you may be missing out on some wonderful instructional allies. But improper use of props can undermine your efforts. What lessons from the stage can help you determine which props might be effective, when, and how?

For example, when lecturers use a table at the front to sit or lean on, at least in the tradition of a staged production, they are using a prop. But how are they using it and how does their use of it affect their teaching? We should all ask the same questions about using lecterns, slides, overheads, or any other props. Being actively conscious about the nature and purpose of the physical objects used in class — props

— can help you eliminate distractions, engage your students better, and enhance their learning.

Consider the following suggestions:

- Examine your use of props. Are you helping your students learn or are you distracting them? You may decide to improve your use of some props and eliminate others. Getting feedback from colleagues or students can help you identify problems and suggest changes.

- Add props that could enhance your teaching; e.g., a laser pointer, overheads, slides, videotapes, or films.

- Improve your use of such a simple prop as the blackboard with some forethought, feedback, and experimentation. Your writing may be small and difficult for those in the last row to see. Perhaps you clutter the board and confuse students that way. Maybe you could improve your diagrams.

- Experiment with using chalk or markers of different colors, to provide your students with some visual help in organizing information.

- Think about other kinds of props for particular topics — a flag when discussing national identity or patriotism, articles of clothing as historical references, a pendulum or pulley when demonstrating aspects of arcs for physics or math, a vintage instrument when telling the story of a particular musician, or food items to introduce new vocabulary in a foreign language class. Timpson and Christine Jones have made wonderful use of outdoor obstacle courses as catalysts for learning about teamwork and risk-taking. Climbing up a 40-foot pole and walking across a beam can be a very memorable way to help students confront their fears and develop self-confidence.

Actors love working with props. A particular prop associated with a character can help to individualize that character for the audience. Consequently, actors often select character props even if they are not specified in the script. Likewise, you could enhance your classroom "persona" with a judicious choice of props, as the Harvard classics professor mentioned earlier made the microphone chord his particular trademark. When Burgoyne taught in a room that lacked a wall clock, she daily brought to class a foot-high, red and yellow Big Ben alarm clock, an eccentricity that students enjoyed.

Actors also appreciate working with props because "stage business" with the props gives the actors something specific to do, reducing performance anxiety and the usual accompaniment of fidgety habits.

Final notes: Whenever you use an animal or child during a lecture, be prepared to be upstaged; these kinds of distractions can be difficult for your students to ignore. Even if you can handle mistakes or failures with relative ease, it's a good idea to practice with each of your props, especially with microphones and audio-visual equipment, particularly when you use a lecture hall for the first time.

Exercises

1. You can begin with an inventory of your classroom needs for chalk, markers, overheads, pointers, slides, computer disks, handouts, and the like. What else is available and how could you find out about it? What else would help? Do other rooms have what you need? Could you get access to them?

2. Review your plans for a future lecture. What props would be good? What would be interesting for your students?

Lighting

Like the classroom itself, lighting is just there. You learn to deal with it, whatever you have. Yet lighting can certainly affect what can be seen on the board or screen, especially from the back of the room. So, you may dim the lights for slides or films — even though bright sunlight may still make it difficult in some rooms at certain times of day. Teachers typically have very little control over the ways in which their classrooms are lit, but we still believe there may be lessons from the stage here for improving the ways we teach.

Lighting for stage and screen receives a great deal of attention. Most theatres, even amateur ones, enlist the help of someone experienced in all aspects of lighting. While written scripts may include some indications about lighting, the director and lighting designer are really on their own. Most often, the lighting designer, in consultation with the director, designs a "light plot" and hangs and focuses the lighting instruments, experimenting with different color filters. Considerable time goes into determining and recording the necessary lighting cues. During the last week of rehearsals, at least one technical rehearsal is devoted to setting lighting levels and cues with the actors on stage.

Stage lighting serves various functions, including visibility, emphasis, and mood. The primary function, of course, is visibility — the audience needs to see faces, sets, and props. However, the lighting designer will modify the lighting according to the need for emphasis. The actor most brightly lit draws the most attention; for example, observe how the follow spot on the lead singer in a musical comedy makes him or her stand out from the chorus.

Note that in theatres today, the darkened auditorium and brightly lit stage direct the focus toward what is happening on stage rather than in the audience. Interestingly, this theatrical convention did not become established until the 19th century; earlier, audiences were more active, even vocal, shouting out approval or disapproval of the performance and often coming to the theatre as much to display themselves and to interact with their friends as to pay attention to the play. Darkening the auditorium contributed to the transformation of the audience into quiet and passive observers. When teachers rely heavily on dimmed classrooms for slides, films, or videotapes, we wonder about a parallel transformation of students into passive learners.

Creation of mood is the most innovative aspect of lighting design. Common sense shows us how the quality of light affects our emotions. Think, for instance, of how a bright, sunny day can raise everyone's spirits, while dull, overcast skies may have the opposite effect. Lighting designers can manipulate the intensity, direction, and color of stage lighting to create a brooding, malevolent atmosphere for Macbeth or a sentimental, romantic mood for a musical comedy love scene.

Stage designers have elaborate equipment at their command; you may see little if any parallel with what you have at your disposal in class. Yet designers in many small theatres achieve impressive effects with few instruments or dimmers but considerable ingenuity. Certainly, the principles of visibility and emphasis apply to teaching and learning. For example, spotlights trained on the podium can help keep the focus on the lecturer. A darkened room can augment the impact of slides, film, and television. Some mixture of lighting may be best for showing the overheads that accompany lectures.

Creation of mood poses a problem in many classrooms. If you have a choice of classrooms, opt for one with plenty of windows and natural lighting, a space where you feel comfortable, alive. Fluorescent lighting has its critics. If you can find a classroom with incandescent lights, grab it! On nice days, consider holding class outside. It's amazing what ingenious and determined instructors can accomplish, both within and outside the formal rules. If your students find the room stultifying, you need to work even harder to compensate for that effect. Also, your enthusiasm in class is quite contagious, conveying your feelings about the material. And if your enthusiasm is depressed by that dungeon of a room ...

The biggest challenge for you may be awareness of what is possible. While considering how aspects of lighting might affect a presentation, you will inevitably look more carefully at the student experience. When Timpson and Chris Jones require student presentations in their teacher preparation courses, they will often encourage their students to be creative, to think first about learning and, if appropriate, to use lighting in different ways. Given this freedom, students often then light the classroom space in new ways and their presentations improve accordingly.

Exercises

1. Take a few minutes and reflect on those lectures you've witnessed that made effective use of lighting. Which lectures have been distracting or otherwise difficult because the lighting was too bright or too dim?

2. Think about an upcoming lecture and what changes you could attempt with classroom lighting, no matter how subtle. Use a penlight for focusing attention on slides and overheads, for example. Get to know all your lighting options. Some rooms, for example, allow you to light the board while dimming the lights everywhere else.

3. Get in the habit of checking regularly with your students about the kinds of lighting that most help them learn.

Costumes

Costume design serves important functions in the theatre. Costumes
help to establish the setting for a play. Costumes also delineate character, illustrating the social and economic status of each role, as well
as the individual's personality and tastes. Costume historians argue
that all clothing is costume. Clothing provides a means of communicating the "persona" or role a person assumes, the way he or she
wishes to be perceived. Actors discover that merely putting on their
costumes helps to transform them into their characters, because they
feel different in the costume. Costumes also affect bearing, posture,
and movement. It's hard to play Queen Elizabeth I in jeans!

So what about you? What does all this mean outside the theatre?

While we don't espouse the "dress for success" philosophy, we do
want to make you more aware about your choices and the potential
impact of clothing on your students. What you wear may affect how
students perceive you. Your clothing can make you a powerful, distant professional or a casual, friendly acquaintance. Everyone notices
and smiles when Halloween gives some teachers and students permission to be more playful and dress in costumes, providing some
relief from the routine of campus life. As you explore the different
roles you play in the classroom, think about your costumes.

If you're working on changing your role, remember — how you dress
can also affect how you feel and behave. A favorite outfit can add a
special touch of personality to the first or last class sessions. Older
and more comfortable clothes may make it easier for you to conduct
a demonstration or to take your students outside on the grass. Their
willingness to join in may also depend on the clothes they are wearing, so your planning should include advising them about what to
expect in future class sessions.

When he's working hard in class, Timpson will invariably have to
take off his sport coat or sweater, loosen his tie, and roll up his
sleeves. At the end he often feels a bit like the great James Brown,
the "hardest-working man in show business," who leaves the stage
exhausted, his jacket draped around his shoulders, in a cold sweat
after a charged rendition of "I Feel Good."

For more insights into the effects of clothing on learning, look at the
evaluations students complete about your classes. Do students see
you as distant and intimidating? If so, might a slightly more informal

style of clothing help? Do your students find you unfair? If so, it may be that your casual clothes convey messages that conflict with your high expectations.

If you're planning on lecturing about someone from the history of your discipline, see if you can use some clothing from that era to give students a sense of the time and place — a hat or wig, a jacket, accessories, make-up, a complete outfit if you can find one. Short of that, try using pictures or even just describing in some detail how this person appeared. The fun you have with this may be quite contagious, adding something to class that textbooks rarely provide.

Exercises

1. Take a few minutes and reflect on those lecturers you've seen whose clothes or costuming added something, no matter how subtle. Were you ever thrown off by what a lecturer wore?

2. Think about an upcoming lecture and what impact a change in your usual "costume" could have. Try some ideas for laughs. We know that students appreciate humor. The resulting variety could provide a counterweight to the serious approach that your course requires from everyone.

Notes

Most published scripts are designed so that actors, directors, and other stage personnel have plenty of room to make written notes in the margins. These become reminders and cues for study and rehearsal. Successful productions are never left to chance, especially when the additional anxiety of performing in front of an audience can block memories and cues unless the parts are *overlearned*. With complete confidence in your command of the material for a particular class, you too can concentrate more on reactions from students — who seems alert, who may be confused, who may have a question, who is prepared to respond, who could use a hint, who might be on the verge of an important insight.

Many lecturers routinely scribble reminders or ideas in the margins of their class notes. These may include last minute updates or comments about current events, ideas about student involvement, responses to questions that arose in previous class sessions, hints about material to be emphasized on the next exam, announcements about relevant activities on campus, and the like.

You could make similar use of marginal notes so that you can remember:

- To ask specific questions at certain points to probe student thinking and promote more active participation

- To wait for students who may need a little more time to get their thoughts together and to express them

- To use a visual — an overhead, video, or slide

- To have students complete a short written response and try to put certain ideas or solutions into their own words

- To poll the entire class on certain issues — "How many of you believe that the best response is _____ ?"

These kinds of notes can also help connect each class to the previous class. While you have been concentrating on preparing for class, your students come from any number of other activities — other classes, home or the dorm, chatting with friends, sleep, eating, studying. Some time at the beginning to remind them of your most recent points and where that day's lecture will go can be very helpful as a warm-up and orientation. You can also note reminders that would apply when you teach that course again — topics that you would approach differently, other examples or activities that could help resolve the kinds of confusions students experienced this time around, and questions that generated good discussions.

Exercises

1. Take out some recent lecture notes. Think about what happened in class. What could you have noted that might have helped in the next class period?

2. After the next class, take a few minutes to reflect on what happened and what you might do differently next time — how you began, what sparked the most interest, where students seemed to lose interest or get off track, what you should revisit in future classes, who participated and who did not, what students learned.

3. Ask around among your colleagues. Find out who takes the time to make notations in the margins of their notes. How do these help?

Impact on Students

In the theatre, a production is not a production until it plays before an audience. While a poor production is quickly forgotten, a good one will engage an audience and a great one is memorable. Unfortunately, there are no guarantees; despite the best of intentions, a good cast of characters, considerable expense, and a lot of hard work, some performances just never catch on with audiences. Hollywood history is full of big-budget, star-studded, box office busts. Consider Michael Cimino's *Heaven's Gate*, Dustin Hoffman and Warren Beatty in *Ishtar*, or *Cutthroat Island* with Geena Davis. At last count, Kevin Costner's megabuck *Waterworld* may break even, but $200 million-plus?

And just as often, there are sleepers, those productions with low budgets and a cast of unknowns that come out of nowhere to spark a lot of audience interest and make a lot of money. *Pulp Fiction* was produced for a fraction of what it has now taken in. *The Crying Game* surprised everyone as did the more recent hits, *Clueless* and *Last Summer*. How about the cult classic, *The Rocky Horror Picture Show* or the black comedy about the closing of the General Motors assembly plant, *Roger and Me*?

The same is true for teaching. Your students will let you know, either directly or through nonverbal signals, whether or not they were engaged intellectually or emotionally. While education should never become synonymous with entertainment, students should be able to expect competent organization of instruction mixed with expert knowledge, concern for them as individuals, and an energetic delivery. Some lessons learned for the stage can be particularly helpful here.

An experienced lecturer can often *read* a class and make adjustments as needed along the way. Fortunately, you are not tied to your lecture notes as actors are tied to their scripts. You can improvise and create as you go, as you sense a need. You can always digress spontaneously and take advantage of moments of special interest. Students, of course, are more likely to remember what grabbed and then held their attention.

Timpson remembers fondly one of his own professors who would briefly stop her lecture when she noticed any drowsiness. This was a late afternoon graduate class and most of those enrolled had already worked a full day. Instead of fighting a problem that was not hers or giving up and droning on and on, she would just stop and get all of the students on their feet for a few stretching exercises. What a terrific way to reenergize a group! Once back in their seats, these students felt much more able to participate more actively.

But how do you know what to do? How do you sense the need? You watch. While you lecture, make eye contact. Don't stay buried in your notes. Listen carefully for sounds that indicate restlessness, for coughing or shifting in seats. If you sense that students are beginning to fade and drift off, do something.

There are lots of possibilities. What we recommend here is that you explore more options as you feel the need. Again, we want to stress the importance of feedback in assessing the need and the results.

For example, you can stop and take a break of some kind. Or you can ask your students to hang in there for a bit longer so that you can finish something, but tell them that a break is coming. You can ask for reactions to the material. You can also stop and provoke a discussion with a question or comment. Or you can shift to some other active option: ask the students to write something in class or to form small groups to discuss key points. You might have a simulation or a role-play. It might be a good time to practice some skill in class.

The fundamental question has to be: What is the use of going on as planned if too many students have disengaged? There are a number of possibilities, but they all begin with your awareness of your students and their degree of intellectual and emotional engagement.

Exercises

1. Try supplementing the more typical end-of-course student evaluations with other forms of feedback. Interview students along the way. Have students periodically take a few minutes to assess particular classes: what worked, what didn't, what could have made the class better. A few reactions scribbled on a sheet of paper can be a simple but effective way to provide feedback.

2. Invite colleagues to attend a class, then give you feedback to complement what you get from students.

Chapter 5
Questions, Answers, and Discussions

Do you want lively discussions? Do you want your students to come to class prepared, ready to engage in stimulating interactions? Can your students overcome their timidity or learn to share center stage in order to join in a process of collaborative exploration? Do you want to feel energized by the questions and discussions which occur in class?

You can have more of what you want — and we think that there are a number of lessons from the stage that can help. From your need to shift roles to the importance of "with-it-ness" — your awareness of student reactions and needs — from a concern for timing and set (mood and environment) to the practice (rehearsal) that your student "actors" will need to perform their roles, you may get a fresh perspective and some new insights through the performance lens.

A stage production, with its script and carefully rehearsed organization, may have more direct relevance for a lecture. However, there are also important lessons here for question-answer interactions and discussions. In addition, we will draw on improvisation where scenes are set but actions are not scripted and the outcomes vary greatly.

Some students clearly feel more comfortable in a lecture format, where they can play a traditional role and quietly record the organized and expert conclusions that you offer. The most pressing concern for these students is typically less about learning and more about figuring out just what it is that you want back on assignments and exams. That is what will determine their grades.

What do you do? How do you and your students get more out of the course, more from your knowledge and experience, and more from their abilities and interests? What options do you have? What lessons from the stage can help here?

Other students, of course, come alive with the opportunity to participate more actively in class. They have the maturity and personality to articulate their ideas and to listen to their classmates. Yet, a few may use the opportunity to compete for attention or power, which may cause others to shrink back because they lack confidence in themselves, their abilities, and what they have to contribute. As mentioned, Tobias (1990) and Belenky et al. (1986) have described the negative effects of an isolating and competitive climate in class on many talented students, especially women and minorities. What is your role here in promoting inclusive discussions? How can performance skills help?

Many scholars agree about the value of active learning in helping students acquire a deeper understanding. Whether in sections, labs, tutorials or the lecture itself, opportunities to apply knowledge, to discuss material presented in lecture or absorbed through the readings, can strengthen learning and reveal misunderstandings. Consequently, it's important for teachers to be able to handle questions effectively and manage productive discussions. We think that the stage has much to offer here.

Of course, some teachers will resist any suggestion that a curriculum already bulging with "what has to be covered" be expanded to include more; i.e., time for questions and discussions. We won't pretend that your choices are easy. Trading a measurable focus on knowledge and product for the more slippery domains of thinking and process can feel dangerous — perhaps like the difference between canoeing on the calm headwaters of a mountain lake versus surviving a kayak plunge through the white-water rapids down below. You may well need to rethink some of your core assumptions about teaching, your goals for your students, and your time and resources. In some sense, less (content coverage) may mean more (and deeper learning).

In truth, these whitewater rides can also be quite thrilling, invigorating, and energizing — and with practice you will gain confidence and skill. Just as actors and directors control the timing and pacing of a production, so can you make your rivers of discussions slow and smooth or rocking and rolling. Once you master the art of facilitation, you can create whatever classroom environment you want — and enjoy the spontaneity and freedom.

Current trends in higher education are pushing for more active opportunities for students, more challenges to think more critically and creatively (e.g., Johnson and Johnson 1994; Lowman 1995; Johnson, Johnson, and Smith 1989; Ramsden 1992; Timpson and Bendel-Simso 1996). Whether you use planned small-group activities or spontaneous large-group exchanges, your teaching will bring special joys and demands. You may have to take on some new roles.

Problems and Challenges

Along with becoming more comfortable when thinking on your feet, you may also need to sharpen certain skills in order to effectively orchestrate these kinds of interactive environments. These include:

- Formulating good questions
- Accepting student responses without necessarily agreeing
- Providing additional clarification
- Challenging students to think critically and more creatively
- Summarizing and synthesizing
- Encouraging participation while discouraging domination
- Managing classroom time
- Providing closure when needed
- Focusing on assessment when appropriate
- Helping everyone stay focused on underlying concepts and goals

Some teachers ask questions only for rhetorical purposes. These kinds of interjections can certainly be useful in challenging students to pause and think. However, some actual questions become rhetorical when students do not respond immediately and the teacher rushes to "rescue" the class from the uncomfortable silence. Good questions always have the potential for stimulating student responses and discussions. But, as with so many good things in life, these may

take time to develop — and sometimes teachers may miss these opportunities. To the untrained facilitator, quiet in the classroom may
feel deadly, but we should fight the urge to ease the discomfort — or
we risk creating a truly deadly situation by killing active engagement.

You can also inhibit student participation when your questions are
mostly "guess what's on my mind." What matters in these cases is
not what students themselves think, but what students think the
teacher thinks. Some students won't rise to this kind of a challenge,
perhaps finding it too reminiscent of the approaches used in elementary school. Other students may perceive too much risk in being
wrong in public.

However, there may also be a control issue here, if you insist on
directing the discussion toward a particular conclusion. Some students may feel uncomfortable in suggesting alternative responses.
Disagreements may get suppressed. Opportunities for deeper and
more meaningful interactions may disappear. Indeed, who wants to
pay attention to classmates when it is the teacher who is the expert
and who controls the exams and grades?

Along with a need to formulate good questions comes the challenge
for you to acknowledge, clarify as needed, and respond to what students say and then to guide further discussion. Common problems
arise when questions from a few vocal and assertive students inhibit
others from participating or when someone raises an issue that is not
of interest to the group. Something is also lost when you miss the opportunity to tap into deeper beliefs and understandings in a rush to
get back on task and *cover* everything that has been planned. Here
again, *less teaching* may mean *more and deeper learning*. As the truism
goes, *covering* often means the opposite of *discovering*.

Of course, every teacher has had to contend with students who can
disrupt a good discussion — those who are really after *attention*, those
who may want *power*, or those *hurdle-jumpers* who only want to know
what is required, what will be on the next exam, and so care little
about the involvement and ideas of their classmates. Dreikurs (1968)
has some interesting ideas for helping teachers understand and channel these kinds of motivations into more constructive directions.

Yet there are other problems here as well, barriers that can limit learning to a surface kind of understanding. For example, some students
need *time* to formulate their own opinions; it be necessary for them to
let the eager achievers take all the initiative. Some students tend to

think through issues quite systematically; they may struggle when the discussion bounces all over, when there is no attempt to follow a certain line of reasoning to a logical conclusion. Others may want to incubate their ideas before hatching anything into the bright and often critical light of a public classroom discussion; understanding how creativity depends upon a period of incubation can help you and your students respect this process.

Even when some students have a response in mind, you may need to provide them with additional encouragement and opportunities, especially when:

- The class is large
- You are rushing to cover certain content
- The students are more introverted or lack confidence
- The students lack the necessary communication skills
- English is not the students' first language

Certainly, some students would just as soon have you do all the work, especially since you are the *authority*, the appointed expert, the one paid to educate them, the one who designs the exams and determines the grades. You may reinforce this role if you repeatedly grab the spotlight and upstage student attempts to construct meaning for themselves, that is, to understand the underlying concepts at a deeper level, one that is correct and congruent with the ways in which they see the world.

Some of your students may be quite complacent about their own learning, enmeshed in what Freire (1970) has termed the *banking* notion of education. In this more traditional notion of education, the primary function of teachers is to get "deposits" of information into the minds of the students. During this process, teachers socialize students into a receptive but fundamentally dysfunctional culture of silence and passivity. This approach to education reinforces student docility. Certainly, some students can feel intimidated by open-ended questions that require critical thinking, while others become anxious when put on the spot to come up with specific dates, names, references, or other facts. But should those reactions inhibit our commitment to helping our students develop the skills needed by citizens in a democracy?

In the face of all these challenges — engaging students, pulling in those who are reluctant while keeping a check on those who want to dominate, facilitating interactions, promoting listening while challenging students to rethink, getting the pace right, making the most out of pauses, getting a good mix of roles, and more — we think you can learn valuable lessons from the stage. From scripts to characterizations, from sets to timing, performers and playwrights have mastered a great deal about building interest and provoking deeper involvement.

Lessons from the Stage

Knowing that you are about to mix it up with students, you could learn more from actors about improvisation, what works and what doesn't. Knowing that many students need some time to digest a question and formulate a response, especially when the material is complex and challenging, you could learn from actors how to develop awareness and self-discipline to allow adequate wait-time. Knowing that many students find it easier to sit back passively, you could learn from actors how to shift roles and move from giving information to facilitating responses.

When concentrating on *through-lines* or *subtext*, the actor keeps clear about the underlying theme — for you, the goals and objectives. Understanding the structure and power of good *scripts*, you could look for ways to add some drama or humor to your class notes, even subtle touches that might help sustain student interest. In many classes, *timing* and *pacing* — key components for performers, but often undervalued by teachers — can affect the success of discussions.

Other practices from the stage might also come into play here. Developing greater *stage awareness* can allow you to be more spontaneous in seizing opportunities in class to clarify concerns and deepen understanding. Your alertness to everything going in class and your ability to simultaneously monitor learning and group dynamics require high levels of *concentration*. Using a process similar to a *rehearsal*, you could explore various new approaches, soliciting feedback from students and others, then implementing those that seem more effective.

As an example of what is possible, consider Ed Landesman (Mathematics, University of California, Santa Cruz), an energetic and caring professor who uses different kinds of questions to achieve different objectives. As he works through a calculus problem on the board, he routinely asks for help from students all along the way: "What's next?" "What does that equal?" Students call out responses very spontaneously. No hands are raised. There's no spotlight on those responding. It's a lively exchange, more like a conversation with a group, and it seems to keep everyone alert and engaged. Landesman uses this approach to check student understanding along the way and sustain attention. At times, he will balance this directive style with more open-ended questions, to allow students to explore their thinking, or he may stop to reflect more deliberately on a particular problem with someone who is stuck. For the observer, this looks like great theatre — engaging, alive yet focused, the pace varying with the content, fast-paced when Landesman works problems, but much slower when he asks "Why?" and calls for more reflective responses.

The national literacy campaigns that have sprung out of Freire's work in Latin America, South America, and Africa are additional examples, on a very grand scale, of the value of more active and empowering models of education, where the relevance of performance elements is evident as teachers moved away from giving information and toward facilitating learning. In Cuba, Nicaragua, and Brazil, in particular, poor and illiterate masses "bootstrapped" themselves upward through involvement in small, interactive, and facilitated study groups of people who build an understanding of written language from oral descriptions of their own life experiences, concerns, hopes, and dreams (Timpson, 1988). Throughout Freire's work is the imperative for the teacher to foster engagement through the use of meaningful material and to avoid giving information, but rather focus on facilitating.

In parallel to this work with literacy and empowerment emerged a very original adaptation of theatre. After Freire published *Pedagogy of the Oppressed* (1970), Augusto Boal began to explore its application to the theatre and wrote *Theater of the Oppressed* (1979) and other provocative works (1992, 1995). Here he described various ways in which actors can use the lives of audience members to generate material for performance. The life experiences of audience members become the focus for improvisations. There are no written scripts, just whatever the actors can coax from those in attendance. Problems are "acted out" by volunteers and an audience member gets to see other perspectives and explore various options. All of this can be very exciting, but a profound paradigm shift for performers as traditional theatre is stretched in new directions. Indeed, this shift parallels what happens when we ask teachers in higher education to step beyond traditional pedagogy and consider the various benefits possible from exploring what happens on stage.

Staying Focused:
Interactions and Through-Lines

Because of the spontaneity associated with asking questions and
fielding responses, you may have difficulty remaining focused on
your "scripted" goals and objectives. You can be easily pulled off
onto a tangent or isolated concern. Questions and discussions can
wander from the central ideas under study and make it difficult for
students to assimilate everything into a coherent, meaningful whole.

There is certainly an important place for the relevant digression or
improvisation, of course, but that's a different issue. Here we want
to help you stay focused on a central idea. Continuing attention to
the through-line (underlying theme) can work much like Ausubel's
(1963) *advance organizer*, which uses a description of the underlying
conceptual structure on the front end to help students organize and
remember the more detailed information that follows.

This kind of awareness can help you determine which questions or
responses should be addressed outside of class, which could be profit-
ably answered by others in class, and which you could use as catalysts
to probe and promote better understanding. For example, some students may raise questions about their responses on a particular exam
question. Unless others share that concern, you may want to handle
this during your office hours. Others may ask about material covered
in previous classes or what is clearly presented in the readings. Here
you run some risk of boring those who have read the material and
want to move forward with the discussion. Your willingness to answer
any and all questions may serve to punish those who are keeping up
with the material, who complete their readings on time, and who
come to class faithfully.

On stage, the through-line helps actors keep their roles clear and
focused through the various plot twists and turns. Attention to the
through-line forces actors to put motivation behind their lines. A
successful performance is not when every line came out as written,
but rather when every line came across as believable!

For a classroom example, consider the gap between your role as an
expert and what students often need from you as a generalist.
Trained to be a specialist, you may find yourself spending a great
deal of time in class as a generalist, working with material that is
quite elementary for you. Yet in your research and at conferences,

you may be functioning at the very highest levels of specialized analysis and debate. Can attention to the through-line help you bridge these two worlds?

We believe that lessons from the stage can help you in several areas. For example:

- Figuratively putting on your "generalist's hat" can help you step outside your expert's role and remind yourself of the basics. Timpson has gotten much benefit from his regular tour of duty teaching educational psychology. This grounding pays off when questions from students in advanced classes or discussions with colleagues require greater breadth — human development, motivation, evaluation — than his more focused interests in alternative approaches to post-secondary teaching.

- Getting into your "facilitator's role" can help you concentrate more on learning. Indeed, much of the new challenge in teaching on campus lies here, in helping students learn more independently.

- Focusing on the core goals and objectives (the through-line) can certainly help you and your students stay clear about course direction. Try putting your goals and objectives on the board at the start of class.

- Developing the kind of *metaconsciousness* that allows actors and public speakers to watch themselves perform can help you better monitor the specialist-generalist gap and sense when one or the other role is required.

Actors, of course, must become adept at switching in and out of character and into new and different roles. Depending on the particular production and the preferences of the director, actors will have a greater or lesser role in developing their own characters. Whatever their freedom, knowing the through-line becomes critical in keeping the performance unified. As they develop their characters, actors may also get to experiment with different actions or delivery. After each rehearsal, directors will then usually provide notes and invite reactions from the cast about new possibilities for the next rehearsal. This cycle of study and focus, alternating with some degree of experimentation and feedback, continues throughout the rehearsal period and even the run of performances.

As actors may perform the same role night after night, they must guard against the deadening effects of boredom, of having their roles grow old. Even the best of plot and through-lines cannot save a stale production. Accordingly, the best actors use feedback from fellow actors and audience reactions to continuously improve.

Like the actor, you can learn to channel your energies through study, experimentation, concentration, self-awareness, self-discipline, practice (with set lines and improvisation), and feedback. And, again like the actor, you too need to keep your performances both focused and fresh. While planning your next class, consider the following:

- Reflect for a bit about your own experiences as a student. What was memorable, effective, intriguing? What was distracting and unfocused?

- Think about what you could borrow from other contexts, perhaps from professional conferences.

- Talk to colleagues about their experiences.

- Solicit ideas from students.

- Staying clear about your through-line (goals and objectives), try a very different presentation of the material, a different approach, a different way to organize your class. You could experiment with a discovery approach, improvising as you go, or use small groups. You could put some of the material in a self-study format or consider a problem-based or case study approach. You could try role-plays, debates, or student presentations. Any change requires time and effort on your part, but it could be a worthwhile investment in renewing your energy and better engaging your students.

Exercises

1. Reflect on a recent period of questions and answers. What was the through-line? Did you stray? How far? Which questions could have been handled more effectively in a different manner? Which responses could have been used as catalysts to help the entire group understand better? To change misconceptions or challenge old beliefs?

2. Take a few moments before your next class to concentrate on your through-line. Highlighting these central concepts and key objectives

in your notes can be helpful as reminders and cues during class. Use Ausubel's notion of the advance organizer to ensure that you are clear at the very beginning of class about the conceptual framework that holds everything together.

3. Keep a journal for a few weeks and note your reactions to your handling of questions, answers, and the through-line. Regular attention can help you become more aware of what you do. Any format for a journal can work; the key is to take time to reflect and write. Later you can review what you wrote, look for patterns and interrelationships, and add comments about your journal entries.

4. Because feedback from students is so valuable here, recruit one or more — perhaps a teaching assistant — to evaluate what happens to the through-line in class. A videotape of your teaching would allow you to do the same.

Lesson Plans and Scripts

Compared with the preparation required for a lecture, you may find that formulating questions or anticipating student responses during discussions is quite straightforward. Actors will use the wide margins in their scripts to jot personal reminders — cautions, cues about timing, places for emphases. You can adapt your class notes similarly.

When you write into your class "script" the questions you plan to ask, you can analyze how each question connects to each lesson's through-line. Just as many actors will work through each of their lines to explore the underlying subtext of thought and feeling that connects to the through-line and explains motivations, you should evaluate your motivation for each question. Which questions ask for specific, convergent answers? Which are more open-ended and divergent? While the former can be useful for checking ongoing attention, the latter may be much better at promoting critical thinking and interactive discussions.

Benjamin Bloom and his colleagues (1956) have developed a hierarchy of thinking skills that provides teachers at all levels with a helpful structure for using and evaluating questions.

- At the lowest level of cognitive demand are questions that ask for information, for specific *knowledge,* and that require relatively simple recall.

- The next higher level of questioning requires *comprehension,* where students must demonstrate understanding.

- The third level is *application,* where students have to use their knowledge and understanding to solve a particular problem, for example.

- The three highest levels (in ascending order) involve *analysis, synthesis, and evaluation*: students must dissect issues, pull from a variety of resources in formulating responses, and judge the soundness of results.

A working knowledge of this hierarchy can allow you to achieve a good mix of cognitive demands in class. For example, some questions at the lower end (knowledge, understanding, applications) can help when getting a class started, reviewing materials covered in previous classes or in the reading, and checking for understanding. Landesman frequently uses these kinds of questions as prompts and probes, to keep his introductory calculus classes moving.

Questions at the upper end of the Bloom hierarchy can provide more of the intellectual challenge that promotes rethinking and stimulates developmental shifts. For example, Landesman will periodically focus on a particular student's struggles and use a very reflective style to promote deeper learning — "You're confused about that solution." By planning and teaching with this hierarchy in mind, you can develop your own ability to exploit opportunities that arise spontaneously.

For a performance, even the most minor character on stage must be engaged in the action of a particular scene to make it all work; otherwise, the energy will dissipate and audience members may lose their focus. Unfortunately, too many classrooms look like staged crowd scenes, with a few eager students getting all the lines and lots of "extras" forming the background.

To avoid relegating some students to passive "extra" roles, you could try the following ways to solicit greater involvement:

- "Prime the learning pump" by having students take a few minutes to write out their responses in class, perhaps sharing these briefly with a classmate before you open up for a general discussion. This approach ensures that everyone has some response and gets to discuss first in a small group.

- Have your students write out their names and some biographical information on index cards at the start of a course. Then, throughout the term, when you want a response to a question, pull a card at random. *Note:* Although this approach may promote greater attention and participation, it may engender some anxiety among students.

Engaging Students and Audiences

We know from the work of Belenky et al. (1986) that the issue of student participation can have important implications for learning, especially when student diversity comes into play. More female students, for example, tend to avoid participating in discussions that feel competitive and judgmental. These students often prefer small group interactions as a prelude to a large group activity. Socialized differently, males more often will rise to the challenge. After analyzing attrition in large introductory science classes, Tobias (1990) reported that a number of talented students, including a high proportion of women and minorities, were discouraged by classes that were large, impersonal, and information-driven, and sought out disciplines in which they could learn in a more supportive, cooperative environment.

We think that seeing instruction from the perspective of the stage could give you some new insights, perhaps by making you more aware of student reactions or more attentive to your instructional through-line. You might also think of the ensemble spirit and the rehearsal process as a model for providing ongoing peer support and assistance to students, both in and out of class.

In turn, restless or rude students can dampen any teacher's enthusiasm, undermining the best of preparations. In response, you may want to dance faster and faster in class, to entertain students who don't want to be there. While you could use theatre skills to serve a notion of "instructional entertainment," that is not our intent. Rather, we hope that this book will provide some effective ideas for interesting your students in the course material and involving them more actively in learning.

Acting companies seek to create an "ensemble," a performance approach that encourages give and take, as each member of the company works closely with every other member to achieve a common goal — the best possible performance. Certainly, actors can be very competitive in pursuing their careers, but when they're on stage, cooperation must prevail. Bonding among cast and crew builds during rehearsals and is cemented by the intensity surrounding performances. The resulting intimacy promotes lasting friendships and trust, which can stimulate creative problem-solving.

Current research on effective instruction indicates that an "ensemble" approach can also work in the classroom. For example, a growing number of teachers are exploring the use of small, cooperative group activities to improve student engagement and participation. Johnson and Johnson and some of their colleagues (e.g., 1989, 1994) have reported extensively on the value of small groups for promoting a more active and mutually supportive context for student learning. Successful small-group work can reduce competitive behavior and promote teamwork among students with very different backgrounds, interests, needs, and learning styles. There are a great variety of instructional approaches from which to draw in designing these kinds of assignments (e.g., Timpson and Bendel-Simso 1996). Of course, successful group activities will require attention, time, and effort, but the benefits of "ensemble" learning often outweigh the losses.

Exercises

1. Try reformatting your notes or outline for a class, to leave wide margins on both sides. Add notes to yourself about pauses, emphases, and reminders about participation. After this class, make additional notes in the margins for future reference. Check with your students to see if your estimates of their level of engagement match what they think.

2. Have someone else review your notes and suggest changes or additions. In particular, analyze the kinds of questions you are asking and your objectives for any planned discussions. Watching a videotape of yourself teaching can be similarly instructive.

Hooking Students from the Start

Hooks for stimulating discussion can run the gamut from a challenging question to a provocative statement about a particular issue, from a hint about what will be on an upcoming test to a straightforward appeal for participation, from a riveting demonstration of some principle to a role-play about a central character under study. Whatever you use, however, you can promote student learning by remaining attentive to the underlying goals and objectives (through-line).

A role wheel, as described below, can prove particularly effective in generating discussion. As we've pointed out, the conflict inherent in drama helps to engage the audience. Role wheels can permit students to investigate issues that generate differences in thought and opinion — for example, tensions over grading policies, ethical issues about cheating or plagiarism, opposition of animal rights advocates to courses requiring dissection, controversies pitting new theories against the traditional canon, conflicts between environmentalists and developers. Your choices for topics may be broad indeed.

To set up a role wheel, you ask each student to find a partner. The pairs of students then form two concentric circles, so that each student stands facing his or her partner. You explain that you will describe a situation that the students are to role-play with their partners, noting that the students should not try to "act" but rather put themselves into the situation and behave accordingly. You then describe the situation, asking each student in the inner circle to play "Character A," while each student in the outer circle plays "Character B."

For instance, you could describe Character A as an environmentalist picketing a nuclear power plant who attempts to stop and recruit a worker just now entering. You then create a conflict with a description of Character B as a worker with a family to support and a lot of unpaid bills from six months of unemployment just prior to getting the job at the plant. (Later on, we provide further examples of role wheel situations.)

After describing the situation, you then allow two to three minutes for each role-play, monitoring the interaction carefully to ensure sustained interest. Although the conflict may be unresolved, you can stop the action and get students to switch roles, replaying the situation from the beginning. After allowing two to three minutes for a role reversal, you can stop again and ask the inner circle students to move one person to the right, so that each student stands facing a new partner. You then describe a second situation and repeat the procedure, including the role reversal. You continue to guide the role wheel through a number of situations (two to five seems optimum, since after five energy tends to wane), then move directly into discussion.

Processing student experiences in the role wheel can serve as a bridge back into a discussion of the original issue. You can begin by asking: In which of the situations did you find yourself most involved? Why? Have you ever been engaged in any conflicts like these? What did you experience when you switched roles? Were some roles more comfortable for you than others? Why? Did any of the situations relate to today's topic for discussion? How?

As "hooks," role wheels have a number of advantages:

- They can be used with classes of almost any size.

- Everyone role-plays simultaneously, so all students participate actively.

- Students are less likely to suffer from performance anxiety, since they're playing roles without any "audience."

- Role wheels can help move issues from an abstract level to one that is personal and concrete. Students experience a sense of how others react to complex and conflicted issues. The role reversal then promotes understanding and empathy with other perspectives.

The key to designing an effective role wheel lies in selecting and describing the situations. Obviously, these must relate to the material under study, illustrate some aspect of a particular topic, and help students make connections to their own concerns and values.

Actors use a similar process of reflection and values clarification to connect with their characters. For instance, it's unlikely that an actor playing Oedipus will have any experience with patricide or incest. But he can search for analogous experiences, an occasion when he realized belatedly that his actions had hurt someone. The memory of both the discovery and the pain can help him empathize with Oedipus when he must confront the truth.

While role wheel situations may not — and should not — tap into such intense trauma on the part of students, an effective exercise can begin with the students' concerns and then connect to some aspect of the topic at hand. Role wheels generate energetic discussions, because students engage with the topic both emotionally and intellectually.

There are other exercises you can use as active "hooks." For instance, Burgoyne encountered the "Cyclops" exercise in a human potential workshop and adapted it to introduce discussion of *Oedipus the King* in script analysis and dramatic literature classes. This exercise involves the various senses in an active and physical exploration of a topic.

Burgoyne begins by clearing an open space in the room and explaining to students that they are all going to play a Cyclops. This creature from Greek mythology has only one eye; students form the monster's single eye by cupping their hands in a circle around their eyes. Since Cyclops was a grumpy, single-minded monster, she asks students to stomp around the room, grumbling and muttering — and growling whenever they bump into another Cyclops.

To enhance the mood, she plays a strident selection from Vangelis' "Heaven and Hell" while the Cyclopes stomp and grumble. Then she stops the action, puts on a "heavenly" cut from the same album, and tells students to close their eyes. Now "blind," students move through the room slowly, taking care not to bump into others but using all their other senses to explore anything with which they come in contact.

Concluding the exercise, Burgoyne then asks the students to sit and discuss their experiences: What did it feel like to be a Cyclops? How did it feel different when you were "blind"? What other senses came into play when you couldn't rely on your eyes? What did you experience? In what ways does this exercise relate to *Oedipus the King*?

Students invariably connect the exercise to the sighted/blind imagery in the play, observing that Oedipus receives many clues to the truth as the play progresses, but ignores them because of his Cyclops-like "tunnel vision." When he faces the truth, his whole experience of the world changes. Physically blind, he must now rely on other senses and on spiritual insight for guidance.

How can this kind of activity be adapted for other classes and different disciplines? To nurture empathy and understanding for people with disabilities, Timpson will also have education students "blind" themselves and experience first-hand what it means — physically, emotionally, and intellectually — to depend on other senses. On a more symbolic level, students who are "blinded" could also get some feel for the challenges faced by researchers who are venturing into the unknown on the frontiers of knowledge. Students can get only so much from discussions or readings. Experiential learning can promote a broader and deeper learning. Give it a chance!

If your classwork requires some trust-building or teamwork — for projects, labs, field assignments, cooperative case study analyses, or problem-based learning — exercises like these can also help to "break the ice" and promote bonding. For example, students can act out various character types who make group work difficult. Exaggerating their characteristics can make for a fun way to illustrate problems that otherwise may be difficult to confront. Everyone in the group will surely keep these character types in mind as they work together throughout the semester.

Exercises like the Cyclops and the role wheel also engage students on a sensory level. Here learning styles come into play, as individual students demonstrate particular strengths or preferences in one or more of the modalities — visual, aural, or kinesthetic (touch). Exercises that use more than one format have a wider appeal. Hunter (1982) has long been an advocate of using multimodal approaches and "teaching to both sides of the brain." You can explore acting textbooks for these kinds of ideas and exercises. (See the annotated bibliography at the end of this book for our recommendations.)

But what if your great idea for a hook fizzles and flops? We can all remember classes when our opening question bombed and we faced a sea of blank stares or some desultory leafing through notes for a clue. Challenged with a dead audience, the stage actor might experiment with changes in timing, gestures, or expressions. Teachers have greater freedom: we can try to improvise a new hook on the spot. Perhaps a review of topics from previous classes or items in the news can help get students engaged and focused. A small-group activity or an in-class writing assignment might get everyone involved and prime the pump. We recommend that you experiment with various approaches for hooking students at the start of class and develop a repertoire of attention-getters.

Exercises

1. Watch one of the television talk shows like *Oprah* and analyze what they do for openings, how they set the stage for the questions and discussions to follow. Their use of hooks should be quite evident.

2. Analyze a recent period of questions and answers in one of your classes. How effective was the beginning? Did you have any kind of hook? If you did, how could it have been better? If not, what could have worked?

The Classroom as Set

During a lecture, students must be able to see and hear you. When you move into questions and answers and discussions, everyone should be able to see and hear everyone else. In fact, participation may vary substantially as a function of "sight lines and acoustics." Straight rows and big rooms can constrain discussions, by channeling interactions through the teacher who must then act as gatekeeper. When students are seated in a circle or around a large table, however, interactions can be more lively and dynamic. Even where seats and tables are bolted to the floor, however, you may be able to adapt your approaches to encourage more interaction and discussion. For example, you can have students periodically discuss their ideas with those seated nearby.

Those involved with stage performances and film put a great deal of effort into designing and creating just the right set or finding the ideal location. With some imagination and effort, you might be able to reconceptualize your "set" to promote better interactions. For example, to maximize participation you could think of your students as "fellow actors" instead of passive audience members. Suddenly the entire room is a set and many more options open up. Augusto Boal worked to reconceptualize theatre in a very similar way, pulling dilemmas out of the lives of audience members and involving everyone in exploring possible solutions.

Indeed, reconceptualizing students as resources for instruction could open up even more possibilities for encouraging and deepening learning. For example, when you encourage your students to make creative use of the classroom space for their presentations, you can tap their reservoirs of ideas. When you use small-group activities, you shift the focus from one large "set" to a decentralized grouping of sets with different casts and crews running in parallel with each other.

Similarly, when you see students as actors, you can bring them into more active exchanges through debates and case study analyses. Like town meetings, when citizens gather to discuss matters of civic importance, classes that function this way can engage students and challenge them to think and rethink what they believe. The ethical, newsworthy, or human issues that exist in every discipline, the stories that surround the movers and shakers, can be a rich source for material here.

Whatever you do with the room, however, your decisions should be grounded in your course goals and objectives, your "through-line." By being conscious both of maintaining that focus and of expanding your flexibility, you are more ready to seize upon opportunities to use other spaces that are available, both on and off campus. When asked to contribute to their learning environment, students can meet the challenge, learn from your lead, and bring their own creative ideas into play. Suddenly, the possibilities and limitations of the class "set" become opportunities and challenges for everyone in the "ensemble."

Exercises

1. Make a list of the most creative uses of the class "sets" that you have experienced. How did these enhance instruction and learning?

2. What could you try in your own classes? What other spaces are available? How could you better tap student ideas, creativity, and energy?

The Roles You Play

When you use question-and-answer and discussions, you will have to play a variety of roles quite different from those required in lecture — and in some ways much more demanding. There is a degree of spontaneity here that you may find difficult. Good public speaking skills may not be enough. The increasing diversity of our students — their differences in background, age, preparation, values, attitudes, etc. — and the increasing concern for critical and creative thinking require teachers to think on their feet and respond to a wide range of questions, to help students bridge their differences and to guide further investigations.

For instance, you may need to provide alternative explanations and examples when students struggle for understanding. There may be times when you do *not* want to answer directly, when you can use a question to probe and spark rethinking. There may be times when you want to challenge the entire class or to call on individuals randomly for an answer.

As you move from formal lecture into discussion, your awareness of the different requirements for each role can help you make the transition. For example, a question-and-answer period may mean setting aside your prepared notes so that you can respond more spontaneously. The focus here will change from speaking (lecture) to listening (discussion). In a discussion, you may also function as a moderator, ensuring that everyone can hear or that everyone understands a particular response or comment, perhaps sampling the entire class for agreement.

When you want to promote deeper learning in a discussion period, however, you may need to do even more. You may want to put on the counselor's hat, for example, and actively promote (teach, model, require) the language of *acceptance*, where someone's first response to a comment is to reflect back what is heard and sensed — "So you believe that ...." You could also help bridge differences by promoting (teaching, modeling, requiring) *empathy*, helping students express their understanding of someone else's experience — "You seem to be very confident/unsure about that comment."

When you work in this mode, the *pace* of class may slow considerably. However, there can be decided benefits here, as students feel more secure about discussing their ideas and reactions openly. They know that their comments will be respected. For example, when dealing with topics fraught with potential for conflict and argument — racism and white guilt, the impact of European settlement on native peoples in Australia and the terribly high rates of health problems and unemployment some 200 years later — Michael Williams (Aboriginal and Torres Strait Islanders Studies, University of Queensland) will routinely use reflective listening and empathic statements to promote a general climate of trust and acceptance in class. While he articulates a core belief in the importance of acceptance as a foundation for building a more tolerant nation, he also models the needed communication skills on a daily basis. The effect of this in class is clearly evident as students find ways to discuss even the most sensitive issues. Feelings get hurt at times, of course, but Williams uses acceptance and empathy as a process to achieve a desired goal of respect, understanding, and appreciation. For him, trusting that this process will work means *staying in character*.

There are times when you may want to restrain yourself from answering a question too quickly, when you should stay in character and keep the focus on the student who is asking or someone else in class: "That's a good question. What do you think? Can anyone else respond?" Your role here would be to challenge students to think more for themselves. You may not want to provide answers as efficiently as possible. You may have to discipline yourself to wait, to look over your class for possible respondents, perhaps to rephrase a question or offer an additional example.

With his curriculum organized around problems (cases that require students to analyze symptoms and signs and recommend treatment), Michael Aldred (Dentistry, University of Queensland) regularly performs a balancing act, between his role as facilitator of learning and the more traditional role as expert. His goal is to get his students as actively involved and focused as possible. He asks. He probes. He waits. He watches. He cajoles. He encourages, "Come on, you can do this." He puts some students on the spot. Occasionally, as a last resort, he jumps up and takes the lead. In the long run, Aldred is quite content to walk this tightrope because he remains convinced that problem-based learning has distinct advantages over traditional teacher-directed instruction when the goal is to prepare professionals for clinical work.

At times, you may also want to *get into character*, to answer as if you were someone you have been discussing. Along with providing some insight into the leaders in your field, this can also wonderfully model the ways in which different people approach problems generally. Just how would this person have responded to a particular question? What might his or her critic say in reply? If students struggle with a problem, you could become one of them as you share the various strategies that you might consider and the frustrations with which you could empathize. All of this can help your students develop critical and creative thinking skills.

You may find that your "lecturer" persona actually works against you in your "discussion leader" function and that a deliberate change of character will help. For example, Larry Thornburg (Veterinary Medicine, University of Missouri) takes himself out of the "expert" role and uses a form of role-play in his veterinary pathology class to stimulate better discussions. Thornburg had found that when he asked students to explain a point in class, they seemed unwilling to risk sounding stupid by offering an opinion to "the expert." In order to combat this perception, Thornburg changed his discussion-leader "character." He placed a toy dog on the table and said to the students, "I'm the client. This is my dog. Explain to me what's wrong with the dog and what will happen to it." In essence, Thornburg reversed roles with his students. Instead of playing the expert, Thornburg took on the role of client and cast the students in the role of the veterinary experts. This role reversal really empowered students, opening up discussion. "Discussions go well now," Thornburg says. "I never ask students to explain anything to me. I take myself out of the classroom completely."

With the potential for lively discussion and debate, these kinds of problem-based or case-study analyses can be great fun and quite challenging. For a wider diversity of participation, you can also experiment with having students play different roles. How would a very creative person respond? Someone who is very deliberate? Someone from a related discipline? A very different discipline?

Role-playing can also work when scheduled as an assignment. In this way, students have the opportunity to research their roles as an actor would do to prepare for a production. Because their peers will be in the audience, the performance aspect can motivate even the most unmotivated student.

Actors expect to develop new roles for every production. Some roles may fit their personalities, but others will not, requiring a "stretch." Actors will study and develop their stage characters. They will try various ideas. They will solicit feedback, directly or on videotape. They will take advantage of rehearsals to practice and refine their roles. To succeed on stage, performers must invest in this kind of preparation as a very conscious process.

Exercises

1. Identify the roles you play in class when you ask questions, when you respond to student concerns, or when you facilitate discussions. What are your strengths? What should you build on? How can you overcome your weaknesses?

2. Recall classes or meetings when you were stimulated by questions, answers, or discussions. What "roles" were being played? How could each have been played better?

3. Now consider your best and worst teachers. What roles did they play?

4. Think about the roles that your best students have played. Were those students active in class? Were they well-prepared? What skills did they have? How could you help other students play those same roles?

5. Assess your skill and comfort in the various roles you have to play in class. Circle H (High), M (Medium), or L (Low) below. Note areas where you need to develop new competencies.

Planning	Rating	Comments
Lecturing	H M L	
Questioning	H M L	
Facilitating	H M L	
Motivating	H M L	
Participating	H M L	
Listening	H M L	
Directing	H M L	
Encouraging	H M L	
Assessing	H M L	
Training	H M L	
(Add your own)	H M L	
(Add your own)	H M L	

The Roles You Could Play

Once you realize the potential for enhancing a deeper learning through question-and-answer and discussions, new roles open up. In each case you can explore the advantages through the actor's keys to success — study, awareness, preparation, exploration and experimentation, solicitation of feedback, and practice/rehearsal. With these in mind, consider the following roles:

Being a catalyst for growth

Knowing that learning and development are processes internal to each student, you accept that you can only do so much. In class you regularly present new material and ideas. You can also serve as task-master, judge, and guide. Students, however, must also play their appointed roles as active, motivated, and thinking learners. In truth, perhaps the most important role for you may be as a catalyst for growth, helping students to assess and deepen their understanding while challenging them to assimilate new information, ideas, and skills. Since active and experiential learning are hallmarks for developmental shifts in thinking, you can look for ways to stimulate your students and involve them actively. (Look at our chapter on the developmental case for drama for more details about this.)

Providing encouragement and reinforcement

Knowing that interactive learning is difficult for some students, you can also do a lot to encourage active participation, by applying behavioral principles and offering tangible rewards to shape student responses. For example, you can thank students for responding. You can celebrate their efforts to understand and build on the insights they offer. You can refer to their contributions in subsequent discussions. You can offer points or a grade for participation.

Nurturing creativity

If you believe that creativity is important and you want to nurture it in your students and in yourself, then there are several "roles" you can play and encourage. (We go into some depth on this subject in the chapter on spontaneity and creativity.)

Promoting effective communication skills

Knowing that success with question-and-answer and discussions rides on the cooperation of everyone in class, you can also promote learning by playing the role of a communications skills trainer. Helping students develop their abilities to listen, to empathize, to negotiate differences, and to resolve conflicts can help them learn more from discussions ... and in every other aspect of life.

Initially, you may hesitate to give up content coverage for these kinds of process skills. However, if the quality of the time available improves, if students can acquire much information through study on their own, which allows you to use class time for interactions that help them learn better, then this kind of investment may prove worth the effort.

Keeping track of time and task

A problem for many discussions involves a loss of time and focus, when questions lead to diversions that yield little of substance for the class as a whole. Here, you can become more aware of the interplay among the various factors that impact learning, including time, goals and objectives, engagement, and participation.

Some teachers will write the day's agenda on the board or an overhead, including the time allotted for each item. Then everyone has a visual guide. Although you are the one ultimately responsible for decisions about time and tasks, students can play supporting roles here, in helping you and the class keep on track by pointing out when the discussion has lost its focus or may be wandering too far afield.

Of course, we must also remind you to allow enough time for discussions, both in terms of quantity and quality. You must allow enough temporal space for your students to think or you may only be skimming the surface and miss tremendous opportunities to help your students understand better and more deeply and to make greater use of your knowledge and experience.

Like the actor, you can develop your "audience awareness." For example, check to see if a question was heard by everyone; repeat it if necessary. It can also be important to keep track of timing, to know how long to stay with certain questions and when to move on. Behind the scenes, the stage manager may be responsible for cueing actors for their entrances. At conferences, a moderator may provide for cues when a speaker's time is nearly up. Many small groups work better when someone serves as timekeeper. If you are having difficulty managing the time you allot for discussions, if you get pulled off for too long on various digressions, you might want to explore some kind of cueing mechanism, such as asking your students to be aware of the concern and to speak up or give a signal if they perceive a problem. They are then working with metacognitive abilities, thinking about learning and acting accordingly.

Exercises

1. Recall a class or meeting where there was a particularly effective time period for questions, answers, and discussion. What roles did the teacher, leader, or moderator play? How?

2. Which of the roles described above could help you? How much of a stretch would it be to expand a particular role or adopt a new one?

Delivery

While your role in a question-and-answer session or general discussion is less "scripted" than for a lecture, ideas from the stage can be useful. Performers use timing, expressions, gestures, movements, and voice to make their delivery more effective. For a more complete discussion of delivery, we refer you back to the chapter on lecturing. However, we have a few specific new points to add here as well.

Timing

We have already discussed some problems associated with timing and some possible remedies. As you become more aware about the role of time in class and as you work to allow more time for students to respond, you should be able to affect both the quantity and quality of learning.

Expressions

Because of the traditional role of teachers in directing learning at all levels, students tend to pay close attention to your facial expressions. For a start, you could learn much by watching a videotape of yourself teaching or getting feedback from an observer. One key to improvement is to become more aware of your expressions and how these may be affecting your students. For example, if you want a relaxed and caring mood in class, you could smile more and show greater empathy for student reactions. If you want to appear enthusiastic about your material, your face could show some urgency, a desire to get on with what you have planned.

Gestures

When students are responding, you can encourage their classmates to listen more carefully by avoiding distracting gestures; e.g., nervous or repetitive mannerisms like playing with a piece of chalk or drumming on the lectern or boards. On stage, ensemble work can be very demanding. Actors must know their lines and actions, behave in believable ways, and avoid distractions while others are acting. It's a cardinal sin for performers to 'up-stage' each other; even slight actions elsewhere can draw audience focus away from where it belongs. The same respect would enhance the classroom environment: you can become more aware of what might distract your students during question-and-answer periods and discussions.

Gestures can also be useful to communicate without words, when you want to avoid disrupting a question-and-answer period or discussion. Instead of asking a student to speak more loudly, a simple pantomime of cupping one hand around your ear and straining to hear can convey the message. Instead of asking for responses, you might look at your students, spread your arms and beckon responses with your fingers. You could request help by pantomiming confusion, wrinkling your face and tilting your head with your hands up. You could feign ignorance about a particular question, shrugging your shoulders with an "I don't know" expression to invite students to respond. To encourage a student to finish his or her remarks, you can use the stage gesture of a cut across the neck or a "let's wind this up" cranking motion. Here again, we encourage you to be sensitive to your students, since some may be offended by this message.

Movement

You can also beware of moving around in ways that might distract your students, such as pacing across the front while a student answers. Just as actors learn to avoid a distracting movement by replacing it with a supportive movement, you could remember to stop to face students who are responding, to model the kind of focus you want everyone to have. Be careful, however, to not be the gatekeeper for all responses. You may want to insist that students address their classmates, perhaps even standing to do so if the class is large, while you observe reactions and find ways to encourage others to participate.

Your proximity to students may also affect interactions. Try moving toward those who are responding. This can create an intimacy that helps to personalize and energize the class. When students experience this more direct kind of engagement, more may come alive. Be aware and sensitive, however: moving too close may intimidate some students.

Voice

How you respond to students can impact the amount and quality of participation. As you encourage them, express empathy, join a heated debate, or clarify a point, your voice could change dramatically in tone, pitch, and volume. Actors study the voice and routinely exercise their range so that they can use the right qualities for their roles.

You can certainly improve by becoming more aware of your voice and by actively exploring your vocal range. Once again, it may help to use a videotape, an audiotape, or feedback from others about your voice.

You should also take care not to overuse any response, no matter how positive. If you invariably use the same response — such as "Terrific!" or "That's great!" — you may appear insincere. You may want to use such neutral responses as "OK" or "uh-huh" to signal that you're listening but not convey any judgment, to encourage a student to continue.

Props

As in a lecture, props can enhance discussion sessions. For example, when discussing the burdens of power for one of Shakespeare's characters, borrowing a crown from the theatre department can add a wonderful visual touch. As students respond, each could try on the crown. As mentioned, Thornburg's toy dog becomes an important focus for student-centered case study discussions in veterinary pathology. As simple as the use of these props may seem, they can prove quite memorable for students. When discussing some aspect of molecular structure, a three-dimensional model can be invaluable. Trying to clarify complex ideas or issues with words alone can be difficult in any discipline. These kinds of concrete representations can be of particular benefit to students who are new to a subject.

Once, during a problem-based learning session (small-group inquiry) in oral biology, when his students seemed stumped about how certain muscles connected to the structure of the jaw, Aldred leapt out of his chair and raced down to his office to retrieve a skull. His students really needed to see and handle the skull for themselves. Indeed, their futures as practicing dentists may well depend on their skills in handling the jaws of clients.

As noted earlier, because discussions are "public" and because a few students may tend to dominate, it may be difficult for some students to get the time and space they need to comfortably express themselves. Then you may want to use an especially effective prop — what some Native Americans call a "talking stick." This can be any object that can be held easily — a small stick, an eraser, a pointer, a book, the microphone in a large class. There is one rule: only the person holding the "talking stick" may speak. This person also decides when to pass on the "talking stick" to someone else.

Using a "talking stick" makes the discussion process more deliberate
and it can certainly change the dynamics of a group discussion. It can
promote better listening. No one is allowed to participate without formal (and physical) permission from the speaker. Each speaker knows
that he or she will have the undivided attention of the others and the
time needed to express his or her thoughts. A pause is no longer an
open invitation for interruptions. Silences can allow for reflection.
Topics don't have to bounce around on the often disjointed comments of those participating. Holding a brief discussion about the
group process can help make everyone more aware of the dynamics
that make for an effective discussion and the choices they have, as
individuals and as a group, about the process for future sessions.

Exercises

1. Take an inventory of the props that you currently use — chalk,
pointer, overhead, books, notes, etc. Now make a second list, of
props that you have seen in use during effective question-and-
answer sessions and discussions. Note the differences between
the two lists. What new props could you consider trying? When?
How will you know if they are effective?

2. Brainstorm other possible props. Do not limit yourself to what is
immediately available. Let yourself dream. Think about the possibilities in various disciplines. What could represent the clash between
the environment and development, between local and mass culture,
between micro and macro economic systems, between intuitive and
more deliberate strategies, between old and new paradigms?

Now go back and see which of these is possible, perhaps just as an
experiment. Which props could you gather or develop over time?
Which might take a request for funding from some campus source?
Which could become part of a larger external grant request?

Warming Up

In preparing for discussions, you can identify key issues or potential
concerns and think about how to address them. You can also plan to
clarify any areas that you feel are beyond the scope of that discussion.

Students will benefit from knowing what parameters if any you set for the discussion, where you feel confident to lead, what topics would require additional preparation or an invitation to others to participate.

You should recognize that students also may need to warm up. It may not work well to raise questions at the outset of class. Students may not be sufficiently engaged, aroused, or interested; they may be reluctant or even resistant. If you start with questions, they may work best as a preview, to prepare them for later discussion, or as a way to provide ideas for them to think and write about.

Stage performers put a great deal of effort into warming up their audiences. For example, rock bands and headline comedians routinely use some kind of opening act. Most plays build up to the first turning point, where the hero's journey takes a turn and the story really starts. Operas, ballets, and musicals typically begin with an overture. In contrast, many films and television shows plunge into their stories almost immediately: there's no need to warm up audiences for performances that are not live! We offer here a few ideas to get you thinking about the ways to get your students started.

One possibility is to have students write a few sentences or so on a question that you want to address. This gives everyone a chance to focus, think, and prepare a response before the discussion begins. You could also have students discuss their reactions among themselves, either with a classmate sitting nearby or in small groups. This use of a topic to "prime their pumps" can help get everyone more involved. Even those who hesitate to participate may feel better prepared and more confident when they can reflect on their responses ahead of time and share these with a few others first.

Some language teachers will also use music to help set the stage and guided imagery to help focus the students, calming the inevitable anxieties that accompany classes that require frequent and public participation. Other teachers will use a review of previous material to set the stage for new learning. Still others will pull material from the news to awaken student interest with a touch of obvious relevance.

Many people notice the consequences when they don't take enough time or effort to get ready, when they feel rushed, scattered, unfocused. Athletes can pull muscles when they don't warm up adequately. Performers certainly notice when a hasty warm-up affects their concentration on stage. Actors also use warm-ups as part of the team-building process. Just as a physical warm-up helps a teacher release extraneous concerns and focus on the class, a physical warm-up can help engage students.

For example, Burgoyne has used warm-ups in courses in dramatic literature and script analysis. She asks her students to stand in a circle, then leads them through a brief routine that includes stretching, "hanging oneself up" (see the Energy Center exercise in our chapter on performance-enhancing exercises), massaging each other's shoulders, and shaking out. She has found the warm-up routine effective in developing a class atmosphere conducive to discussion. Warm-ups get everyone going — especially when you are combating sleepiness in an early-morning class or postprandial lethargy in an early-afternoon class!

Some students, however, hesitate to participate at all, whatever you do. They may be shy by nature or anxious about speaking out in front of a large group. They may worry about sounding stupid. Some always seem unprepared for class. Others like to think through their ideas carefully and rarely find the time or nerve in class to come up with responses or questions on their own. Although a warm-up could help here, these kinds of participation problems may require much more systematic attention throughout the course.

Exercises

1. Think of activities or events that have required you to warm up. What was the benefit? The risk when you didn't?

2. Make a note to warm up, on your calendar or in your appointment book. A few stretching and vocal exercises in your office can help, as can a short but brisk walk, perhaps on the way to class. Even if only for five minutes, concentrate on your physical and emotional preparation and note the impact on your teaching.

3. Note what happens if you have to deal with student questions or equipment problems before class. Does your energy evaporate? Or early in the semester, when things are most unsettled, is your energy excessive?

Reactions from Students

Awareness of students becomes especially important on two levels. On a micro level, you have to deal with the individual question that someone raises and the responses that result. On a macro level, you need to be aware of what the rest of the students are doing. Here you should keep in mind the group focus, how you can pull other students into a question. You can help engage them mentally and physically by calling for a show of hands — e.g., "How many of you had that same question?" — or doing a spontaneous, short writing exercise — e.g., "Let me ask each of you to put a few thoughts or feelings down on this question." To a writing exercise, you could add a small interactive activity — e.g., "Now I'd like you to turn to a classmate, share what you have written, and see what you have in common."

Problems

We expect students to behave responsibly in class; to a large extent, they do. However, we must remember that the changes they are experiencing in their lives are dramatic. They now have much greater control over their time, commitments, life style, relationships, finances, etc. They often make the decision of what campus to attend, what area(s) of study to pursue, what elective courses to take, when and how to study. Since our students and/or their parents are paying for at least part of their education, they can be expected to act more like customers.

All of these choices and changes inevitably affect what happens in class. Many students have outside roles and responsibilities, such as jobs and families. Many suffer from insufficient preparation, poor motivation, lesser abilities, and/or other adjustment difficulties. When teachers use a traditional lecture approach, most student problems go unnoticed; in more active environments, such as question-and-answer situations and discussions, however, individual difficulties can really stand out, sometimes in the form of behavioral problems.

When such problems arise, try basing your appeal to the students in question on respect for those classmates who are trying to learn. Empathizing with those who are attempting to juggle much too much can help build trust and open communications. You can always ask disruptive students to stop or leave.

Some students may need some guidance, assistance, and insistence from you to pay attention when their classmates speak. After all, they may think, how could student comments ever appear on the exam? You can certainly draw their attention to good questions and comments and, when appropriate, signal what could appear on a future exam, e.g., "That's a point that could work on a quiz" or "That gives me an idea for the midterm." At times, you could even remind them to listen. As mentioned, you could also engage them with a poll or a short writing assignment followed by a discussion.

As mentioned, it's very important to act proactively, to be conscious of the need to keep a *group focus* as much of the time as possible and to plan for a variety of engaging activities. If you can keep the attention of your students, if you succeed in building on their responses and questions, you should minimize behavioral problems.

So go for it! Take some chances! Try some discussions in your biggest lectures. Vary the format in your smaller classes. Experiment with role-plays and debates. Explore your own roles. Work at being more aware of the dynamics involved in a successful discussion. Push beyond your comfort zone. Step off into some new directions. You expect your students to get into new areas and to take risks; you should at least dare to do the same, to show the same spirit of adventure.

Chapter 6
Energy, Creativity, and Spontaneity

Despite the best of intentions and regardless of the extent of your preparation, you can never predict exactly what will happen in your classroom. Of course, you should be current with the latest information and the newest ideas in your field. Of course, you should have your material organized well, sequenced carefully, sprinkled with relevant examples, etc. However, you can always benefit from developing your ability to think on your feet.

Teaching in higher education requires expertise and often a very narrow specialization. Yet, the best teachers also possess other qualities, vitally important in meeting the needs of students. Of these, energy, creativity, and spontaneity are three of the most vital.

In the often hyper-rational arena of academia, mention of these kinds of qualities often raises eyebrows. Some of our colleagues may even be quite critical of a quality like spontaneity in a culture seemingly driven by demands for analysis and proof. When energetic and creative teachers receive high ratings from students on evaluations, some colleagues may deride these results as "pandering to students" and little more than a "popularity contest."

Some of our colleagues also criticize students today as being inferior to those *in the good old days*, as having less self-discipline and motivation, as coming to campus with fewer skills, underprepared for what lies ahead, numbed by television, and hooked on drugs, sex, rock 'n' roll, etc. — it sounds a lot like the '60s and the complaints of the previous generation! Critics who make such assumptions are likely to expect students to choose entertainment over substance and to give lower ratings to teachers who stress learning. Yet, the evidence is quite to the contrary — students are remarkably reliable in assessing the quality of teaching (e.g., Marsh 1987; Andrew, Timpson, and Nulty 1994.)

Moreover, when pressed, many of these critics will admit that teachers should be energetic and responsive, especially when the material seems dry, when students raise questions, or when a discussion begins. When pressed, many critics will also admit that teachers should do more than give information and "prep" students for exams, that they should attempt to inspire.

Even the best material can get lost with poor delivery. We believe that all of us can do more to ensure deeper learning by getting past the minimalist notion of subject coverage and challenging students to think critically. When you raise your expectations in this way, then the instructional value of energy, creativity, and spontaneity becomes more clear. Understanding how performers breathe life into their scripts can help you get more of these qualities into your teaching.

Improvisation and Spontaneity

The word "improvisation" may strike terror into the hearts of many teachers. "What about my notes? My preparation? My expertise? My students expect, even demand that I be organized." Of course!

Yet, certainly there are times when it is necessary to change direction, when students are disengaged, when your examples just don't work, when a particular question sparks a lively exchange and you want to go with that flow. You can learn to do so through activities that make you think on your feet and explore new possibilities. While actors are grounded in their scripts, they too can benefit from work with improvisation when developing their characters, exploring their stage relationships with others, or working to keep their performances fresh.

As Viola Spolin, author of *Improvisation for the Theater*, points out, "Everyone can act. Everyone can improvise. Anyone who wishes to can play in the theatre and learn to become 'stageworthy' " (1983, 3). Routine performances can appear unnatural, disconnected, mechanical, and labored. Training and practice with improvisation can help inspire performers and allow them to act more convincingly, to explore their relationships with others on stage, and to make their roles more "natural" and believable. Along with various arguments for improvisation, Spolin includes numerous exercises. While we offer some ideas here for you to try, you may profit from reading her book in its entirety.

Working with improvisation can give performers, especially amateurs, refreshing breaks and periodic reminders about the joys of acting, dancing, and singing. Teachers can also benefit from taking a break so as to explore new possibilities and renew their interest in teaching. Students will certainly respond positively to your energy and enthusiasm. Just as important, improvisational exercises can also help stretch your creative abilities and develop your flexibility to react to whatever may happen in class.

When getting a staged production ready, actors will often work out their relationships with each other by experimenting with ad-libbed lines, gestures, expressions, and movements. The key is for them to explore a range of situations and possible reactions. Good acting requires much more than delivering lines and actions on cue. It's really about creating believable characters and memorable roles. Dropping a line or missing a cue can be forgiven so long as actors stay in character and the show goes on. Rarely does an audience even know when lines have been "blown." The ability to improvise in character has saved many actors and many shows.

Dancers as well need energy, creativity, and spontaneity. Periodic sessions or workshops devoted to improvisation can help nurture the expressive creativity that underlies success on stage. For example, dance teachers will call for their students to perform ideas and feelings on the spot, through movements, postures, gestures, and expressions: "Be a machine. Now tell a story without words. Be happy, sad, silly, fastidious, cranky, tired." Freed from the need to match music to set moves or to synchronize precisely with others, dancers can explore what lies within them. This kind of opportunity to express their feelings can help dancers add energy and creative inspiration to the development of a final production. Are there lessons here for teachers?

Applications in Class

Periodic opportunities for questions or discussions, for instance, can give teachers a chance to use their creative and spontaneous talents.

Here, teachers can free themselves from over-dependence on their notes and engage their students more directly in exploring the material. The resulting shifts in focus and interactions can energize you and your students.

As mentioned, Tobias (1990) has criticized traditional strategies that emphasize information acquisition and competition in large introductory science courses in particular. She investigated "talented dropouts" who started as science majors, but then switched over to other disciplines, where they were quite successful. Many of these students were women and/or minorities who reported feeling discouraged, isolated, and unmotivated in these competitive, impersonal classes. Indeed, most students do better when they can interact and have the support and assistance of peers.

Recognizing this, Peggy Delaney (Ocean Sciences, University of California, Santa Cruz) blends a careful organization of content with ongoing sensitivity to student needs for clarification, assistance, and involvement. She maintains a focused but relaxed pace in her lectures. She comes to each class with specific goals and objectives, but then proceeds to teach in a measured, flexible, and open manner. Accordingly, students can raise questions or add comments at any time. Delaney will stop, respond, and then check for other reactions before moving on, engaging her students in a series of running conversations. She never hurries, smiles easily, and seems to welcome all questions.

Delaney wants to avoid what she calls the "firehose" approach to teaching, where students are blasted non-stop with information. To better accommodate the needs of her students, she seems to adjust her expectations easily as she goes along. She wants her students to think in class and tries to channel her enthusiasm into a concern for their learning. Indeed, students may well have to do more on their own outside of class, but the knowledge and confidence they gain in class should allow them to work more independently later. Delaney is very approachable and frequently attracts a crowd of students at the end of class who want more from her.

In contrast, Michael Warren (Literature, University of California, Santa Cruz) uses a more traditional but fast-paced approach to lecturing. He schedules regular breaks during class for more spontaneous interchanges with students — questions, comments, discussions. While some students may prefer a slower pace overall, these breaks allow everyone to catch up and think a bit. Most students seem to be thoroughly energized by Warren's lively enthusiasm. To us, his style feels like interval training in track, where sprints alternate with jogs and time for recovery.

When you engage in these kinds of spontaneous interactions, you want to concentrate on picking up important nonverbal signals and other indications, often quite subtle, that students are confused or struggling, that they're bored, anxious about an upcoming exam, or just tired and needing a break or a change of pace. As you reflect on your teaching and explore various approaches, you will become more aware of such signals.

How can you put more energy, creativity, and spontaneity into your classes? Consider the following possibilities:

- Concentrate on listening more carefully to student questions and take time in class to explore underlying confusions.

- Capitalize on issues that excite your students, relevant items in the news.

- Try debates and role-plays.

- Invite someone to class who has some special expertise and can spark new ideas. With you serving as facilitator — fielding questions, summarizing the points made, or suggesting new possibilities — and watching for audience reactions, your guest can be a very effective catalyst for deeper learning.

- Help build on what gets said, relating ideas to what emerged in previous classes or what appeared in the readings.

- Play the classic devil's advocate role and look for points of controversy or disagreement: Who can offer an alternative solution or explanation?

- Search back in time or project off into the future: What was the prevailing paradigm a hundred years ago, a thousand years ago? What will it be a decade from now?

- Probe deeply into particular issues and values and consider how others might respond: What would the critics say? What would scholars in related disciplines say?

Here is an example of a discussion format that may be widely applicable. Michael Williams (Aboriginal and Torres Strait Islanders Studies, University of Queensland) leads his classes with a similar kind of openness and sensitivity to student needs. For him, this becomes

especially important in the context of cultural differences, where in-
digenous students in Australia often feel intimidated by the hierarchi-
cal, critical, and information-driven nature of many university classes.
In hopes of encouraging his students to understand their own thinking and develop their own voices, he fosters an open and accepting
climate in class that minimizes judgment and encourages participation.

For example, Williams was once leading a discussion on a traditional
Aboriginal story in which a cockatoo gets to speak to a human. For
many of us in the room, thinking about the validity of the story was
proving to be a dead end. Just what was its "real" significance? What
did it really mean to the members of the tribe who have passed it on
over the centuries? What did it mean to members of other tribes?
After patiently listening to a variety of interpretations, Williams suggested that "perhaps this issue is really unresolvable and we have to
accept that."

The classroom discussion then took a very important turn that
touched on feelings just below the surface. In response to these
comments about story interpretation, how different people will find
different meaning, a more general discussion ensued about the validity and usefulness of labels generally, for any group. Williams asked,
"When thinking about the responses of others, does it make any
sense to generalize about the ways in which non-Aboriginal people
will interpret this story? What white Europeans will say? Are these
categories so big that no sensible conclusions can be reached?"

You see, some of the white students in the class were feeling both-
ered by the labeling that put all of them into one large, amorphous
category, yet many were nervous about raising the issue directly.
Later it turned out that some of the Aboriginal students had a similar
concern. Their perceived differences reflected differences in tribal
identity, geographic origins, life experiences, personality, and the like.

Here, Williams was able to make a very effective connection with
the issues raised in both discussions; i.e., that we may have to accept
as fundamentally unresolvable these larger questions, the "true"
interpretation of the legend and the validity of any generalizations
about large groups. His skill in gently focusing this discussion
seemed simultaneously to allow everyone to move to a better understanding while addressing deeply felt concerns.

Michael Aldred uses a similar student-centered approach that generally draws on his energy, creativity, and spontaneity. He advocates a
problem-based approach for preparing dentists, insisting that the
more traditional lecture approach to covering course material does
not do enough to promote a deep understanding. Accordingly, he
now lectures as little as possible, relying instead on his ability to raise
questions, probe responses, and facilitate discussion. In a rapid-fire
style, Aldred asks and prompts, "What's going on here? What do you
think? Who wants to have a go? C'mon, you can do this. What's the
first thing you notice? Look at it. Think. Use your common sense."
There is no formal "script." The focus is on students and their abilities to analyze various cases and explain their conclusions.

Enhancing Creativity

There is a certain looseness to these kinds of improvisations, a looseness directly connected to creative expressiveness. You might expect
that by design any formal "training" in creativity would be free-flow-
ing and non-prescriptive. Some activities are indeed like that, while
others are quite structured.

Viola Spolin, a founder of American improvisational methodology,
argues (1985) that certain environments and structures promote
creative behavior:

An environment that encourages personal freedom:
Our culture, Spolin observes, inhibits creativity because individual
feelings of self-worth are regulated by our need for approval from
authority figures and our fear of their disapproval. For creativity to
flower, an environment of trust must be established in which the
individual can explore freely without dependence on the approval/
disapproval dynamic.

A structure that focuses all energies on problem-solving activities:
Spolin finds a model structure in games, which focus energies upon
achieving a specific objective but encourage creativity. Games allow
individuals to *discover* how they can best reach their goal — there's no
one "right" way. Like a game, an improvisation is not chaos; there are
rules for each exercise. Thus, improvisation paradoxically unleashes
spontaneity while teaching self-discipline, as participants willingly
work within established boundaries and concentrate on solving a
problem rather than on winning approval. Concentration provides the
key to problem-solving; indeed, Spolin emphasizes this relationship

by calling the specific objective for each of her theatre games the "point of concentration."

A structure in which individuals learn through experience and develop their awareness of self, others, and the environment:
In fact, Spolin (1983, 3) asks us to consider that "what is called talented behavior is simply a greater individual capacity for experiencing." In order to experience the world, we must find the courage to engage it totally and directly — with our senses, our intellect, and our intuition — instead of accepting definitions handed down to us by authority. "Spontaneity," Spolin insists, "is the moment of personal freedom when we are faced with a reality and see it, explore it, and act accordingly" (4). In the fullest sense of the term, improvisation is experiential education.

Self-Awareness

As is true for many, you may be your own biggest barrier to innovation. Your fears and inhibitions, your perceptions of social norms and taboos, may block you. Performers use improvisational exercises and role-play to sharpen their self-awareness, to help them see their self-imposed barriers more clearly. For example, as they walk around in a circle, a director or choreographer will call out, "Be small. Be big. Happy. Dumb. Disconnected. Salty. Run. Stumble. Be lazy. Surreal." The focus is on responding freely to the unusual, on stretching and exploring. Plus, it's a lot of fun. After becoming more consciously aware of their blocks, these performers can push out and explore new possibilities.

The same is true for teachers. Here is a good example. K, a professor of earth sciences, wanted help because of student complaints that his classes were boring, routine, dry. He had taken Timpson's workshop, "Teaching as Performing," in the hope of getting some new ideas. On the end-of-semester evaluations, too many of his students would remark that K didn't seem to care about his material or about them. When Timpson asked about this, K expressed real frustration, insisting that he truly loved the material, that he always had, and that he found these comments from students troubling.

The problem seemed to reside primarily in his sense of a "professorial" self. His mental image was one of objective expertise, dignified and remote, rooted behind the lectern. Over time K came to understand the effect of this role on his relationship with students, the distance that they felt, their equating his dignified, remote demeanor with dry and routine instruction. Gradually, K became more aware of the ways in which he had been suppressing his enthusiasm in class. With feedback and encouragement, he began to experiment with a more relaxed and caring presence; he gave himself permission to share more of his joy and excitement. As you can well imagine, his students responded positively, further reinforcing K's desire to change.

Exercises

1. Some language teachers try to lower anxieties and thereby enhance learning by relaxing students at the start of a class. By playing music softly and dimming the lights to show slides, by using a quiet voice and a slow cadence, and by asking students to close their eyes while the beauties of the native geography are described, these teachers promote an increased receptivity to learn. (See "Suggestopedia" in Timpson and Tobin 1982.) You can try something similar in your own classes, perhaps for a few minutes before an exam, when reviewing key concepts or clarifying what you want with answers.

2. For dancers, *isolations* are exercises that promote a heightened physical self-awareness. A choreographer will ask dancers to rotate one shoulder independently of the other or each in opposition to the other. They'll try to move their chests from side to side independently of their hips. Try these exercises. With some exploration and practice you too can develop a higher degree of bodily awareness. This consciousness can then carry over to the classroom and help you both eliminate distracting behaviors and add movements and gestures that will be congruent with your words.

3. Augusto Boal, author of a number of books on the application of theatre practices for non-actors, likes to begin with what he terms *demechanization* exercises, which are intended to break routine (habitual, unthinking) movements and reengage the senses. Try this: With your right hand, trace a perfect circle in the air. Put that hand down and with your left hand trace a perfect square in the air. Stop that. Now try to do both at the same time. Reverse directions.

Notice the concentration required to attempt both at the same time. Imagine what you would notice in class if you were this attentive to the nonverbal messages going around, yours and your students'.

Creative Expression

As a teacher you have a wonderful opportunity — a license, even a mandate — to create and innovate. If students become bored and l istless, are you able to adjust your plans and do something to energize and reengage them? If students come to class unprepared or you find yourself with some extra time before class ends, can you come up with something spontaneously? Unlike actors, you are not bound by any slavish adherence to your *script*. Admittedly, you may find it challenging to come up with something that works on the fly. However, spontaneous shifts or digressions can make a difference and renew student interest — questions, personal anecdotes, a role-play, an impromptu debate. When student learning is the objective, your goal becomes much more than coverage of the material and your options (and obligations) can increase dramatically.

Actors must recreate and reenergize a production every time the curtain rises. Creative expression is part of what brings a written script to life. Without that energy and concentration, productions can be flat and lifeless. In the rehearsal process, performers have the time and space — and responsibility! — to explore possibilities and polish performances. Getting a production ready for opening night is both exhausting and exhilarating, requiring the kinds of stretching and discipline so important for the creative process. Every production needs overall leadership from the director/choreographer/conductor, study and effort from the performers, and support and assistance from the stage crew.

However, every production crew — whether on a Hollywood film, a big Broadway musical, or a high school production — struggles with limitations of budget and time when they are trying to create sets and costumes. Creativity becomes doubly important for maximizing the resources available. Beyond these juggling acts, actors will often continue to refine their roles throughout the production's run, making minor adjustments to their roles, to their delivery, movements, and gestures — all the subtleties that make performances sharp, energetic, and believable.

Whenever we see a new production of something we have seen before — Shakespeare, a musical, a remake of an old film classic — we inevitably feel the tendency to compare one performance against the other. Accordingly, performers and directors feel a challenge to add something creative. For instance, every serious Shakespearean actor must think long and hard about the options for delivering Hamlet's famous dilemma, "To be or not to be: that is the question." Just where should the emphasis lie? On "to be"? On "not" or "that" or "the"? On "question"? Multiply this decision by all the opportunities for artistic interpretation and you quickly understand the importance of creative expression.

The same imperative holds true for teaching. Your emphases can help direct how your students learn. The silences you provide can create a space for reflection. The activities you design can promote critical and creative thinking. The subtleties you note can help you cue into student struggles and what might prompt new insights. Your enthusiasm can inspire their commitment.

Whatever the discipline, we all share a need to promote creative thinking and expression. The future may well belong to those who can envision new solutions, form new alliances, cooperate across cultures. More concretely, how can we help students respond to the increasing press of technology into the workplace? What can you do in your courses to encourage creative use of technology? What software makes sense? Can you substitute for traditional assignments, perhaps with multimedia projects that students could create combining text with graphics, photographs, slides, animation, video, film, and sound? Can your students be linked to you and each other through email discussion groups?

A Whack and a Kick

Along with the various exercises described here, we can also recommend several books on creativity itself. For example, Roger von Oech has written two wonderful and popular books, in a very light, readable, and straightforward manner. You may find much of value here, a good place to begin a more focused study of creativity — both for your professional activities and for your personal life.

In *A Whack on the Side of the Head*, von Oech (1983) discusses the locks that confine our minds:

- The insistence on the "right" answer

- A preoccupation with what is assumed to be logical

- A conforming impulse to follow the rules

- The call for practicality

- The pressures to stay on task

- The avoidance of ambiguity

- The fear of making mistakes

- The prohibitions against play

- The commandment to be serious

- The assumption by many that they lack creativity

von Oech insists that we can all open these locks.

Exercise

1. Your awareness about the qualities that underlie your creativity can be a good place to start your study of creativity and its applicability to your work. Using your experiences and understanding, rate yourself on the six qualities below, adding comments in the space provided:

Quality	Rating	Comments
Self-awareness Being able to understand your own strengths and limitations, your needs and goals, your reactions to events around you, etc.	H M L	
Creative thinking Innovating, introducing new possibilities, etc.	H M L	
Being present Concentrating on the task at hand — teaching, learning, questions, responses, the time remaining, the group's needs, etc.	H M L	

Quality	Rating	Comments
Reflecting Thinking and writing about your own experiences, reactions, feelings, concerns, relationships, etc.	H M L	
Spontaneity Feeling free to digress, feeling confident in your own awareness of what is happening and what changes would be helpful, etc.	H M L	
Risk-taking Willing to take chances, to explore new possibilities, to learn, etc.	H M L	
Implications for teaching How have these six qualities affected your teaching? Your success in facilitating student learning?	H M L	

In his sequel, *A Kick in the Seat of the Pants* (1986), von Oech describes the four roles that typically constitute the creative process — explorer, artist, judge, and warrior. Each role represents a set of behaviors and attitudes that you can use in work situations — exploring new approaches, preparing new courses, researching new topics, interacting with students — or for personal growth. Because von Oech's roles are not scripted, they have a definite improvisational and creative quality to them.

As an *explorer,* you need courage to venture into uncharted waters, perhaps to try a new approach. You may need to collect lots of ideas and be willing to rethink certain assumptions or beliefs. You give yourself permission to break out of ruts, to analyze and overcome self-imposed fears. You may even look inside yourself for new ideas, tapping your intuition and creativity. Indeed, you may prove to be your own best adviser. Ideally you enjoy — or learn to enjoy — this process of exploration.

At this point you may want to pause and reflect upon the following:

- What explorations could help you stay energetic and creative as a teacher? For example, is your commitment to course coverage limiting your ability to explore new and more engaging possibilities?

- Is your use of knowledge-based exam questions (e.g., multiple-choice, true-false, matching, fill-in-the-blank) emphasizing too much surface learning (i.e., memorizing, cramming, regurgitating)?

- Are your classroom activities routine — habitual and uninspired?

As an *artist*, you should imagine what may be possible, according to von Oech, and look at an issue or problem from a reverse angle, from a different vantage point, through different lenses, from a performer's perspective perchance! Metaphors can help. For example, how might teaching be like conducting an orchestra or directing a film? The *artist* learns how to break rules when necessary, how to fool around, how to let thinking roam and ramble — all of which can help to generate fresh insights.

Pause and reflect for a moment on the following:

- When are you an artist in your teaching?

- What more could you do?

- When do you go more with your own intuition?

Especially when you try some of the more active, performer-based approaches that we recommend in this book, you may need to shift your judgment about success from the purely objective and the quantifiable (e.g., paper-and-pencil exams) to more subjective assessments of deeper learning and creative thinking (e.g., observations about the freshness of responses given).

As a *judge*, von Oech suggests that you will need a critical eye, an analytical perspective. On stage, success depends on countless decisions, big and small. Similarly, in class thousands of decisions form the environment for learning. Consider the following questions:

- How do you decide exactly what to say and when?

- How do you break bad habits and develop better approaches?

- What readings do you require? Then, what do you need to say about each?

- How good are you at evaluating student responses and assignments?

- How consistent are you?

- How fair are you?

- How well do your graded assignments match your learning objectives for the class?

- How do you know when a class is going well?

- How do you decide what changes to make?

- What values do you bring to class? What expectations? What biases?

Finally, as *warriors,* von Oech wants you to put a plan into practice. Certainly, analogy has its drawbacks, but it suggests taking action and fighting for what you want. For the stage, rehearsals point everyone involved toward opening night. In your planning process, you can point toward getting everything organized for that first class. Staying with this analogy, you can also think about the "weapons" you have to attack ignorance and lethargy in class, your "defenses" against student preoccupation with grades, and the various "strategies" and "tactics" that you might use to promote greater student engagement and deeper learning. Take a moment to think about your strengths as a teacher/warrior.

Exercise

1. von Oech identifies various "locks" that confine our minds. Evaluate yourself (High/Medium/Low) on each of the following. Reflect on the implication of each for your teaching in the space provided:

Mind Lock	Rating	Comments
How important is a "right" answer? Are various solutions possible?	H M L	
How important is logic in your assessment of student learning? Are feelings or intuition permissible in their reasoning?	H M L	

Mind Lock	Rating	Comments
How important are your requirements? Can students suggest alternatives?	H M L	
How important is it for you to always be practical as a teacher? When is the whimsical appropriate?	H M L	
How important is it for you to constantly stay on task? When are digressions useful?	H M L	
How important is it to avoid ambiguity? When does complexity make definitive answers problematic?	H M L	
How important is it for you to be serious? When can you let go in class, get (appropriately) crazy, and have some fun?	H M L	
How important is creativity to you? Where does creativity stand in your hierarchy of course goals?	H M L	

Synectics

Beginning in the early 1960s, William Gordon's seminal work has attempted to tease out those aspects of creativity that are foundational, generalizable, and trainable. In what he coined as *synectics* — from the Greek roots *syn* (to bring together) and *ectics* (diverse elements) — creativity becomes a quality that people from all walks of life can understand and use with practice. Here, creativity is not some mysterious quality, limited to a very few areas like acting or the other performing arts. Instead, it is a process and a quality that anyone can apply ... and should.

As Toffler and other futurists continue to remind us, creativity should become increasingly important, for example, as technology takes over more and more routine tasks. On campus, computers have already proven their value as powerful tools for crunching numbers and processing words and connecting people around the world. Gordon recommends that anyone interested in nurturing creativity begin by being open to possibilities and free to explore — qualities long valued, in particular, by actors, playwrights, jazz musicians, performance artists, experimental filmmakers, and choreographers, among others.

Following this lead, you can look for evidence of creativity in your own field.

- Who were the giants, the trailblazers?

- Who are the free thinkers today?

- Who was able to venture forth against the odds, in defiance of conventional wisdom and the prevailing paradigms, and really push forward a particular field?

- How did they think and function?

- How did research and progress proceed?

- What were the blocks, the blind alleys, the false leads, the popular but misguided ventures?

- How could more free, open, and creative thinking have advanced your field?

Answering these questions can help you and your students tap a motherlode of useful examples. We think that Gordon is right. Creativity is everywhere; you just need to have the right mind-set to see its manifestations.

Cultivating the creative can also mean celebrating some aspects of *non-rational* or *quasi-rational* ways of knowing, those that are more intuitive, perhaps requiring leaps of faith or deriving from sudden insight, musings, and dreams. Most actors certainly use every means available — studied and imagined, analytical and intuited, reflective and impulsive, original and stolen — to make their roles more believable and alive. In academia, the history of every discipline is packed with examples where *non-*, *quasi-*, and *hyper-rational* processes were all involved and at different times, in breakthrough research, creative initiatives, and paradigm shifts. We believe that effective instruction requires a dynamic mix of preparation and spontaneity. The best teachers routinely rely on their intuition to "feel" the need for a change in plans or to gain fresh insights.

Every class has a unique life of its own, with a special mix of experiences, personalities, abilities, motivations, and expectations. Thinking through all these variables to plan for a course of study is difficult in the most relaxed of times — and often overwhelming when they collide in the classroom, when decisions must come in waves — how to say this or that, what information to give with what emphasis, whom to involve and when, how to answer which questions and when to move on, etc. The truth is that we must rely upon a variety of means — rational, quasi-rational, and non-rational — to find our ways through complexities. As we do so, Gordon urges us to be more consciously aware of the creative process.

To cultivate the creative, Gordon recommends regular exercise and stretching for your mind and senses. He likes the use of metaphors for *making what is strange appear more familiar.* When introducing a difficult and complex new concept, you can use concrete metaphors to give students a better foundation for understanding theories and abstractions. For example, the concept of *creativity* we are describing here could be likened to the bonding of cast and crew into the kind of cohesive *team* needed for a successful stage production. Different personalities, talents, motivations, and experiences become connected in an intricate web of overlapping relationships and interdependencies. Just think of your own experiences with groups where individuals were able to subordinate their differences and capitalize on their collective talents in order to achieve a common end.

Gordon also argues for helping students *make the familiar strange,* for turning ideas or problems upside-down and inside-out, looking at them from different and perhaps fresh perspectives. For example, you can look at your classroom as a *theatre set.* Can you see new possibilities, new arrangements of the seats and desks to encourage different kinds of interactions, new uses for the wall space to display the results of small-group brainstorming, changes in lighting to spotlight a guest speaker or to dim the room to encourage quiet reflection?

Finally, Gordon urges regular *practice.* If you value creativity, then you can promote it in your teaching and assignments for students. Practice, the repetition of new behaviors, is akin to the rehearsal process so central to any staged production. Typically, the more performers rehearse, the more they are open to exploration and feedback, the more creative they become. In your teaching, you can look for places to stretch your thinking about what and how you want students to learn. Consider taking unique and unusual perspectives or requiring students to make creative input into class assignments where appropriate.

When Timpson assigns a group presentation in one of his education classes, he often insists that students try to add some creativity. Although he deliberately leaves this expectation open-ended, he gives them several examples of projects that he believes had creative elements. For example, some students have dressed in costumes and used role-plays to make a point, some have invited guest speakers to spice up a discussion, some have mixed in video clips or music, and others have actively involved their classmates as participants. Given this kind of expectation, many students will rise to the challenge and introduce fresh and engaging ideas or activities. Most students seem to enjoy the process of dreaming up something new and different, and everyone seems to enjoy the resulting variety in the presentations. With this kind of assignment, Timpson also articulates his support for the creative process in general.

Focusing on the Present

Performers must concentrate on "being present." Practice with improvisation and role-plays, for example, can help them become more able to overcome distractions, to convert scripted lines into believable dialogue and prescribed blocking into natural movements. To do this, actors need both independent study and rehearsal to go along with their concentration and energy.

It has taken years of study and experience for you to develop your subject area and instructional expertise. As with performers, it also takes considerable energy and concentration to stay "present" in class, spontaneity to respond effectively to students and their questions, and some creativity to guide learning in ways that challenge assumptions or expose new insights — all of this happening, of course, while you watch the time you have available and try to monitor student engagement and reactions.

Gerry Delahunty (Linguistics and English, Colorado State University) tends to move quite quickly through course material, but pauses regularly to watch for student reactions, to provide additional *wait time* so students can process complex material, to understand any confusions they might have, and then be able to raise appropriate questions. Delahunty uses this *focus on the present* to guide the challenge he sets for students. One student likened Delahunty's class to an hour's worth of intellectual push-ups — high praise indeed!

Although you may feel pressured to cover lots of material, at what cost does this occur when student attention and energies are flagging? You may well find that a short and energizing diversion could produce wonderful dividends for learning.

Exercises

1. Many people, teachers and performers alike, derive great benefit from a variety of meditative practices. Whether it's a mantra or yoga, Tai Chi or swimming laps, the repetition of a word or action allows the mind to focus and relax. Concentration can be vital for the teacher. Experiment with the following:

- Take some time, perhaps 15 minutes twice a day, to quiet your mind, focus inward, and achieve a state of relaxed alertness.

- Take a few minutes before and after class to stop working and quiet yourself in a similar manner.

- Use your walks to and from class to clear your mind of distractions.

- Use exercise — jogging, swimming, biking, lifting weights — to achieve the same mental calm.

2. Good communication skills also require you to be more present.

- Practice listening more carefully to what students, colleagues, and friends say to you.

- Practice reflective statements, in which you rephrase what someone has just said and, perhaps, note their feelings.

- Concentrate on understanding others before launching into your own stories, explanations, and interpretations.

For example, after any exchange you can rate yourself (High/Medium/ Low) and reflect on your skills as a listener on the following criteria:

- How well did you keep the focus on the speaker's issue
  and keep your own opinions on hold?   H M L

- How well did you reflect back the speaker's message?   H M L

- How well did you reflect back — observe, sense —
  the speaker's feelings?   H M L

Ask the speaker to rate you on these same criteria. Compare your results and analyze the process. Share ideas and feelings.

3. Acting teacher Robert Benedetti (1976, 11) gives the following simple "Here and Now" exercise as the second step in his training program for performers: "Put yourself at rest. ... While breathing comfortably, say to yourself sentences describing your immediate awareness. For example, 'Right now I am lying on the floor, I am doing exercise #2, I am making up sentences, what will I do first, my right hand is a little cold,' and so on. Do this as long as you can."

This may sound like a simple task, but most beginning performers find that their minds wander quickly away from the "here and now." With practice, the actor learns to stay in the present and then to "allow the sentences describing the endless present to fade gradually away, leaving only a restful alertness." As Benedetti points out, "Relaxation and concentration are two aspects of one state of mind and body."

After you have tried this exercise, record your reactions in a journal. In what areas could you improve your teaching by being more focused on the present?

4. Mirroring exercises form a staple of actor-training, both for effectively developing concentration and for engendering interpersonal sensitivity. In the basic mirror exercise, two performers stand facing each other. One initiates movement, while the other "mirrors" the movement as precisely as possible. The movement may be abstract (for instance, slow sweeps of the hands, turns of the head, bends of the knees) or concrete (for example, a pantomime of brushing one's teeth).

The point is not for the initiators to "fool" their partners with unexpected movements but for both to move simultaneously. The initiator quickly learns that slow, rhythmic movements are easier for the partner to mirror. Periodically, the acting coach calls out, "Change." Then, without breaking the flow of the movement, the initiator becomes the mirror and vice versa.

As a second step in the exercise, partners mirror in front of a group and try in this case to fool the audience as to which of them is the initiator and which is the mirror — a goal that further heightens concentration. With practice, the partners become so sensitive to each other that the coach can ask them to move together, each at the same time the initiator and the mirror. (For specific details on this and other mirror exercises, see Spolin (1983), *Improvisation for the Theater*, pages 60-62, 66, 75-76, 175, 234-35.)

Experiment

In the classroom, the time invested in these kinds of improvisations and role-plays also allows for other possibilities, for experimenting when students struggle with a particular concept or when maintaining their engagement requires a change. As with any such attempt, you can allow yourself a certain freedom to fail and, consequently, to learn. Understandably, you may well feel some discomfort, some confusion along with some success, as well as some uneasiness about straying too far from your original plans, the text, or a more conventional approach. Students are generally very understanding, however, especially when your motivation is to support their learning. If you want to improve, you can enjoy a wonderful freedom to experiment.

Consider enrolling in an adventure course, a ropes course, an Outward Bound experience, or the like where the focus is on experimentation and risk-taking. These can be wonderful experiences for personal development and, when done with a class or with colleagues, for team-building and bonding.

Reflect

Personal reflection about teaching is often helpful, but especially so after you've tried some innovation. Certain questions prove helpful when you change direction and try something new in the classroom:

- Was the experiment worth the time?
- What was gained? What was lost?
- Would more time help? Less time?
- Are more guidelines needed?

Exercises

1. Research on teaching has identified a factor that Kounin (1970) first labeled as "with-it." This is the ability to be alert to what is happening in class and to make appropriate decisions on the spot, such as when students are confused or disengaged or when there are enough complaints about an exam to warrant reconsideration of the grading. These kinds of situations require skill at spontaneous decision-making.

Reflect on the improvisations that you've had to do in various classes. What worked? What didn't? Why? What options are worth exploring?

2. Keeping a professional journal can do much to help you become more aware of your energy, creativity, and spontaneity. Excerpts might also prove useful when documenting your efforts for a teaching portfolio or otherwise making your case for an annual review or for promotion and/or tenure. Here we note how journaling can fit into Seldin's (1993) description of possible materials for a teaching portfolio.

Consider the following questions for guiding your journal writing:

- How was your energy today for teaching? For other activities? Explain.

- How creative were you feeling today for teaching? For other activities? Explain.

- How spontaneous did you feel today for teaching? For other activities? Explain.

Chapter 7

An Introduction to Development, Discovery, and Drama

Learning is orderly and predictable. Knowledge builds in a sequential, stair-step manner. Teaching is about effective delivery. Students should be quiet and reflective. Instruction should be systematic and carefully sequenced, much like the scientific method. Maybe!

Indeed, some of the best teaching and most profound learning experiences can be spontaneous, inspired, and energized by the challenge of questions left unanswered. Ideas and personalities mix, tumble, and sometimes collide in a complex and interactive dance. New work on chaos theory or the nature of the universe, for example — or any books about the history of science, for that matter — remind us that our knowledge is tentative and that our attempts at understanding are uncertain. Debates about human development and intelligence further frame our general lack of knowledge within a context of what we don't even know about ourselves as a species.

In these next two chapters, we want to claim benefits for performance training far beyond enhanced delivery, energy, creativity, and spontaneity and to connect with two major lines of research on student learning. We contend that ideas drawn from the performing arts can enhance the intellectual and emotional *development* of students as well as their abilities to address problems and engage in the *discovery* of solutions.

We will make two cases here: one for turmoil, conflict, and "drama" as developmental catalysts for intellectual and emotional growth; and the second for discovery as a "dramatic" way to capture more of what is exciting and revolutionary in every discipline. We will describe the ways in which performance ideas can help you challenge students to clarify their values, broaden their thinking, and deepen their understanding as well as help you use the great discoveries to engage and inspire.

Chapter 8
The Developmental Case for Drama

A large and growing body of work describes the stages through which students pass on their way toward more independent and sophisticated systems of thought. In addition to the benefits that the stage offers for generally engaging and energizing students, you can also use drama to capitalize on anomalies, incongruencies, tensions, disagreements, and differences as catalysts for inspiring lasting change on a more personal level. The drama inherent in debates, for example, can help spark individual growth, challenging students to rethink their assumptions and to develop more sophisticated methods of analysis and problem-solving.

Background

As children, we think in very concrete and egocentric ways. As we mature, we gradually develop a greater ability to handle abstractions and logic, to mediate our thinking with symbols (e.g., language, mathematics). When we are very young, we learn about the world primarily through our senses. As adults, we become less dependent on direct experience and better able to learn through reading, discussion, thinking, and imagining. There is a similar developmental process on an emotional level.

On a moral level as well, we can find a parallel developmental progression. When young we usually think in terms of obedience and duty, fear and punishment. Over time we develop a greater concern for our relationships with others and more principled reasoning based on ideas about the collective, social good and what we believe is right. As we develop as individuals, we do learn to think and feel in qualitatively different ways.

While the changes that occur through childhood are profound, the changes during the late teens and early 20s are perhaps less obvious but equally dramatic, perhaps more so. Although initially limited to rather narrow and dualistic thinking, students inevitably move toward a greater ability to understand and accept complexity (Perry 1981, 76-116). Throughout this life journey, drama as we are defining it can be a powerful catalyst through which teachers can stimulate learning and challenge the ways in which students think.

Conflicts on Stage

In the theatre, actors look for conflict to heighten audience engagement and sharpen the focus on core issues. As Shurtleff (1978, 43) insists:

> Conflict is what creates drama. Plays are not written about our everyday lives or the moments of peace and placidity but about the extraordinary, the unusual, the climaxes. I am always surprised at how actors try to iron out the conflict that may lurk below the surface of a scene, flattening it instead of heightening it. Perhaps we are taught so thoroughly in our everyday lives to avoid trouble that actors don't realize that they must go looking for it. The more conflict that they find, the more interesting the performance of the play.

Classroom Climate

First and foremost, a climate of *acceptance* and *trust* is vital if our students are to respond to our efforts to engage them, if they are to participate more actively, if they are to open up and be honest about their thinking, about their ideas and doubts, and about their efforts to understand the material. If students are to volunteer more in class, if you want them to take more risks and feel comfortable enough to disagree and debate, then *encouragement, rewards*, and *psychological safety* become important.

There is an underlying developmental journey that moves students from a preoccupation with their peer group toward greater independence as learners and individuals — intellectually and emotionally. A similar journey moves young people from fear of the unknown and outright prejudice toward understanding, tolerance of differences, and even appreciation for the strengths in human diversity. In these developmental journeys, it's important for teachers to understand the role that drama can play.

Peer pressure can be a powerful deterrent to student motivation, learning, and personal change. Students may not agree with certain ideas or judge them to be "politically incorrect." If you want to exploit more dramatic conflict in class, you can insist that your students practice acceptance and understanding. If need be, you can play the devil's advocate and be purposefully provocative, portraying a particular point of view to help bring to the surface minority or unpopular views. In this way, you can help students better understand other perspectives and approach new or different ideas with greater tolerance.

As in the theatre, there may be a tightrope for you to walk when you tap into deep hatreds and destructive prejudices. You must be aware of individual sensibilities and public mores whenever you entertain the controversial. However, knowing the place for tension and conflict in promoting the development of critical and creative thinking will help you to decide what to use, when, and how.

Here is another example of a constructive classroom process that regularly surfaces differences of opinion. Timpson has facilitated many sessions for faculty who want student input about a course early enough in the semester to allow for improvements. At a teacher's request, he will visit a class to ask students for their appreciations, concerns, and recommendations. There is often some real drama here, as students make public statements, both positive and negative, about the course, the teacher, the readings, the assignments, etc. At times there are disagreements. However, this kind of a structured process has proven to be very useful both for teachers and for students, who appreciate the opportunity to give feedback.

You can certainly do something similar for your own classes. You can invite someone to facilitate this kind of feedback process, then leave class to encourage a more open discussion. However, you can also do this face to face. Timpson will commonly interrupt his courses about a third of the way into the semester, often after the first exam, to spend 30 minutes or so to solicit feedback directly. What happens then has some real drama, as students play out very new and empowering roles for them, discussing and debating suggestions for improving the course.

Promoting Engagement

We also want to reemphasize the value of student engagement as a foundation for intellectual and emotional transformation. Armed with new ideas and skills from the performing arts, you can become a more effective catalyst for student development and deeper learning, provoking when students are passive or disinterested, drawing on comments or examples, questioning and challenging, facilitating discussions and debates, creating role-plays, scheduling guest speakers or trips, videotapes, films, or slides, and so forth.

One strategy is to use the notion of *group focus*. A stage production will not succeed if only a few members of the audience are hooked. Being more conscious of your students as a group can help you keep an entire class more engaged, for example, by turning questions or comments from a few into forums for others to participate. You can also take a moment now and then to poll the entire class — "How many of you agree with that?" Turning the class in these kinds of directions can help pull students out of passivity and get them to respond actively.

As another way to promote greater student engagement, some teachers will ask students to help them develop exam questions. Having students participate more in decisions about assessment may increase their motivation to learn.

In some of her classes, Burgoyne will use the review days prior to the exam to have students bring questions they think should be included on the test. Then, in small groups, her students discuss and refine their questions. Later, members of each group present to the whole class what they believe to be the most significant questions. The students' choice of questions shows Burgoyne what they consider important in the course material, what analytical skills they think they should have developed at this point in the class, and so on. She finds that most students take this process seriously; many of their questions are ones she would have asked, but others stimulate useful insights for her as well as for the class as a whole. Then, when they see their own questions on the exam, students also recognize that she values their contribution.

Diversity

Mixing a focus on drama with a developmental view of students and learning can also allow you to do more with the diversity in your classes. On stage or screen, differences among characters can produce obstacles and tensions, adding believability and spice to the plot as it unfolds. Accepting the place of constructive conflicts in your classes can help you reframe problems into potential catalysts for student growth and deeper learning.

For instance, differences of opinion about a topic or solution can be extended into a discussion or full debate. You can probe student thinking using lots of "What if ...?" questions. You can refrain from pronouncements of what's right or wrong and let the uncertainty motivate your students to dig deeper and think for themselves. For developmentalists, exploring student errors can be a much more effective approach to understanding and resolving learning problems than the more conventional focus on correct answers.

Effective Communications

Your communication skills become very important for capitalizing on the potential for classroom drama. Using *reflective listening, acceptance*, and *empathy*, you can help students *think* more for themselves. Whether working as a team on a project or helping each other through a problem set, students can improve their communication skills and achieve lifelong benefits. When students interact with others to test and assess their own ideas, they can sharpen and deepen their thinking. Conflict or drama arises from those interactions, when students have to both listen and explain within the same conversation, when they attempt to understand and persuade at the same time.

Accordingly, you can promote this deeper learning by teaching and practicing the fundamentals of good communications. You can start with *reflective listening*, where students learn to focus on others, on helping those speaking clarify their intent. Instead of quickly giving an answer to a question, you can challenge your students to think more deeply by repeating their concern, perhaps rephrasing, and then asking for their ideas. "Wow, that's an interesting question. What do you think? Does anyone else want to comment?"

When students work in small, cooperative teams, for example, and develop an interest in their classmates, they inevitably deepen their understanding of the material and improve the chances of successful team results. Reflective listening is one very necessary skill here.

It can be just as important to teach and practice *empathy* and *acceptance*. These qualities are essential when students work on cooperative projects or in groups. Here you focus attention on understanding the feelings of others and respecting their experiences. You can help students reflect on how it must feel *to walk in someone else's shoes*. The class focus then shifts away from a sole pursuit of the right answer toward greater interest in developing critical and creative thinking skills and deeper learning.

These three components of effective communications — reflective listening, acceptance, and empathy — can help break down resistances, convert differences into stimulating exchanges, resolve conflicts, negotiate compromises, and open students up to new ideas, viewpoints, and possibilities. As such, these skills can be useful across the various disciplines, especially with the increasing interest in group work and teams as alternatives to traditional lecturing.

For example, we now know a great deal about the benefits of study groups, especially for students in large, demanding introductory science courses where there is a great amount of information to be mastered. Some teachers will help students form study groups, where these communication skills become important for their academic success. For example, Timpson has offered additional credit to students who will study together and then submit a brief written analysis of the impact. Many students value this opportunity and some quickly realize benefits, enhancing their learning as well as improving their grades. He has also encouraged groups that have formed around a class presentation to meet outside of class and help each other prepare for exams.

Admittedly, concentrating on communication skills will take some time, but the investment could pay off in the long run, as students may understand more and at deeper levels, giving you higher-quality instructional time. Moving in this direction can also give you some wonderful opportunities for new dramatic possibilities. For example, students could productively role-play any number of situations relevant to the organization of your class:

- A group project breaks down when one member is unmotivated

- A class discussion goes nowhere because one person is dominating

- A discussion becomes uncomfortable because some students are fearful of comments that could be labeled "politically incorrect"

- The teacher returns exams and several students want to contest their grades

Focusing on such issues can help you promote greater understanding as well as resolve conflicts among your students. The possibilities are infinite. As we have suggested, you can even enlist students to meet with you in a collective effort to improve the course before the semester ends. With good communication skills, you and your students can explore problem areas in an open and constructive manner, then consider new possibilities.

Active Learning

By bringing together a feel for the dramatic and a developmental orientation, you can also increase active learning. Within a performance paradigm, for example, you can see your students either as members of an audience or as members of the cast and crew, each playing a vital role. As audience, they are engaged intellectually and emotionally. As cast or crew, they must take a much more active role. We agree with the developmentalists who insist that it may be more in the cauldron of activity — thinking, practicing, solving, applying, creating, producing — that students can best make course material meaningful and understandable for themselves and each other.

You can encourage active learning in many ways:

- Design active experimentation into a laboratory assignment.

- Require a group project for class.

- Make time for discussions and debates.

- Stop a lecture and have students discuss an answer in pairs before you move on.

- Arrange for field experiences such as internships and practica.

- Organize tutoring or cooperative study experiences.

As with the development of communication skills, the possibilities for active learning are endless.

The classroom drama here means a switch for students from a purely receptive mode to one where they must actively participate and construct meaning. For instance, they may have to overcome inhibitions or fears to interact with others or help with a presentation. They may have to confront an external reference (e.g., you, some other expert, the text, a video) and argue for their own interpretation. This kind of "drama" can have a profound impact on learning, affecting students on a very deep and personal level.

For another example, we note that the latest paradigm shift in science and mathematics education involves an effort to operationalize inquiry and induction, to reinvent the instructional process with students as "workers" *constructing* their own knowledge. Five related "E" words may help you remember the key concepts here:

- Engage (learners in learning)

- Explore (new content and processes)

- Explain (to students and colleagues)

- Extend or enrich (deepen learning)

- Evaluate (periodically check on progress being made)

When we refer to *constructivism*, we mean that students must try to make sense of the course material through connections to their own experiences. As Davis and colleagues (1990), Yager (1991), and others suggest, constructivist teaching and learning involve complex interactions, open conversations, discussions and debates in which hard questions are asked, substantive ideas are engaged, and anyone can be called on to justify an interpretation.

Again, we find the performance tradition offers relevant skills and strategies. Playwrights and directors rarely confront an audience directly with moral conclusions. From a developmental perspective, it's invariably more effective to challenge people with dilemmas and let them rethink their own positions.

For *Twilight: Los Angeles 1992*, a powerful and provocative play about the Rodney King beating, trial, and resulting riots, playwright and actress Anna Deveare Smith interviewed a wide range of people close to those events — a gang leader, a former police commissioner, a jury member, a realtor from Beverly Hills, a community organizer, the editor of *The Los Angeles Times*, Sen. Bill Bradley — 50 in all — and created a script from those interviews. She used the words of these people to bring each character to life through a series of monologues and conversations, addressing the audience directly as well as the other characters. Weaving a complex tapestry of perspectives, reactions, and values, Smith offers no simple solutions, only complex and troubling realities.

Set during the years surrounding the breakup of the Soviet Union, the play *Slavs* paints a similarly complex picture of reality. Tony Kushner juxtaposes the idealism of the socialists and the "cultural genius of the Slavic people" with the environmental devastation epitomized by the nuclear accident at Chernobyl. As with *Twilight: Los Angeles 1992*, *Slavs* ends without any easy resolution, but a challenge — the actors turn from the action on stage to confront the audience — in the form of Lenin's famous question, "What is to be done?"

Once again, we note the parallels to Perry's (1981, 76-116) work on the cognitive development of college-aged students: thinking moves from a dualistic right-or-wrong orientation in the earliest stage to a greater ability to understand different perspectives and accept complexity.

Social Context for Learning

Developmentalists also encourage group learning wherever possible. On stage, the interdependencies of cast and crew provide a rich milieu for creative ideas, support, and feedback. In class, lively discussions and small-group activities can help students see how their ways of thinking compare. In general, developmentalists recommend that teachers organize a stimulating and challenging environment, and then facilitate engaging student interactions. The classroom drama here is relatively straightforward. Instead of concentrating solely on delivering content, look for opportunities to use a more social context — small-group activities, games, simulations, role-plays, cooperative projects, field trips and assignments, and the like — to promote engagement and stimulate learning.

What's important is your attention to the *process* of learning — the skills, attitudes, and feelings that students need to make the most of these kinds of experiences. At a skill level, it all begins with good communications.

For instance, the Campus Writing Program at the University of Missouri-Columbia encourages teachers of writing-intensive courses to incorporate peer review of rough drafts of papers into the class structure. Written materials help students focus on specific aspects of the paper: thesis sentence, organization, quality of insights, etc. Just before the first in-class peer review session, Burgoyne and her teaching assistant hand out to their students a sample paragraph. They then use that paragraph as the basis for a role-play of the oral part of the process, in which the peer reviewer gives feedback to the paper's author. This particular role-play also includes demonstrations of how *not* to give feedback.

In the role of peer reviewer, Burgoyne may say: "This is a terrific paper. I wish I could write as well." In the subsequent discussion of each role-play, she will ask the class, "Was that helpful feedback? Why or why not?" "No," students will invariably reply, "because it wasn't specific. The reviewer didn't give the author any suggestions on how to improve the paper."

As peer reviewer, the TA may say, "You're wrong in your analysis of Hamlet's character. He's really hesitating to kill Claudius because he's not sure the ghost was telling the truth." "Was that helpful feedback?" Burgoyne asks. "No," her students would reply, "because there are lots of ways to interpret any play. The reviewer needs to help the writer make a clear case for the writer's interpretation and not impose the reviewer's."

As the role-plays proceed, the teacher and TA show how to give specific feedback in a constructive, encouraging way and how the paper's author can seek to clarify these comments through paraphrasing and questioning. Students find this role-modeling more engaging than any lecture on feedback. They also enjoy the role-reversal of seeing their teacher in the role of student author, accepting feedback and discussing strategies for improving her writing.

Our Challenge to You

The developmental journey that characterizes the college years may be the most profound across the entire life span. These years and experiences reflect major transitions toward greater independence and produce dramatic changes in thinking. At any level — local, regional, national, and global — a greater ability to work with ambiguity and complexity may mean the difference in whether or not humans can live in harmony without destroying the planet. While higher education may become increasingly important for providing the intellectual leadership for progress, the performing arts can teach us much about the place for drama in engaging hearts and minds and imagining new possibilities.

Chapter 9
Discovery and Drama

As a teacher, your command of the knowledge base in your field is as important as your ability to sequence ideas and convey your material in an engaging manner. Students at all levels appreciate enthusiasm, clarity, and organization. By helping students with the interconnections among ideas and facts, you also help them remember better.

However, do you ever say much about the stories of discovery, the processes that produced the knowledge? How did the greats in your field think about the problems they faced, what they did not know? How did they overcome obstacles and frustration? How were their ideas incubated and developed — or discarded?

Given the pressure to cover a lot of material, you may feel compelled to concentrate exclusively on the end products, the "facts" and proven (?) theories. You may feel you have little time to address any stories of discovery. Yet, these dramas can help capture and sustain the interest of your students, providing an important counterweight to the flood of information from lectures and readings. These stories can also convey much about critical and creative thinking, then and now.

Think about it. Just what is the half-life of a degree these days, especially in the sciences or engineering? How soon will some of the information you provide prove wanting, ultimately to be replaced by new ideas, language, or paradigms? In our "Information Age," students cannot possibly learn enough in four, five, or six years to succeed indefinitely in their careers and their lives. It's increasingly more important that they learn how to access knowledge and how to use it.

In Charles Dickens' *Hard Times* (1854, 5), the archetypal austere headmaster, Thomas Gradgrind, describes to a visitor an extreme preoccupation with facts so characteristic of the nineteenth-century British schoolroom:

> Now, what I want is, Facts. Teach these boys and girls nothing but Facts. Facts alone are wanted in life. Plant nothing else, and root out everything else. You can only form the minds of reasoning animals upon Facts: nothing else will ever be of any service to them. This is the principle on which I bring up my own children, and this is the principle on which I bring up these children. Stick to Facts, Sir!

Gradgrind is a caricature, of course. But that preoccupation with facts and more easily measurable knowledge — which may perhaps have suited a social structure that used schools, in part, to *civilize* children from the poor and working classes to meet the labor needs of an expanding industrial society — continues to dominate many introductory courses in higher education, especially in the sciences. But times have changed since *Hard Times*. Our workplaces are incorporating technology to replace routine labor. Society demands far more critical and creative thinking of anybody who wants to do work that is fulfilling and meaningful. If change is the name of the game on all fronts — work, home, leisure, community, personal — then we may need new and different educational paradigms.

As Bob Dylan, the poet laureate for those of us who grew up in the 1960s, foretold: For the times they are a-changin.'

We believe there is much potential for the use of drama in higher education — if you want to go beyond a recitation of the facts, if you want to promote a deeper understanding, and if you want to showcase the creative and critical thinking that inspired the breakthroughs in your discipline. Look for those conflicts, tensions, and dramas to engage your students and challenge them to think.

Scholars bring along a lot of knowledge, skill, *and* baggage to their work — their training, the known knowledge that defined their own years as students, their current theoretical assumptions and life experiences, as well as their hopes, dreams, ambitions, biases, and the like

— all the stuff that makes them professionals and human. Differences of opinion are inevitable, predictable, and part of the rich tapestry of thinking that defines human inquiry and progress. When observations and statistics and events can be interpreted in different ways, do you take full advantage of the diversity of opinion that may exist? Do you address the different opinions in your classes? Or do you shy away from disagreements and conflict?

And what of the challenge, the "drama" when you ask students to do more to discover solutions on their own? One reason for the remarkable endurance of the lecture format is that it will always be simpler and more efficient for teachers to give explanations than to help students come up with explanations on their own. Think of your favorite Agatha Christie, Alfred Hitchcock, or Sherlock Holmes mystery. Are you any good at figuring out mysteries? Some authors and film directors are experts at maintaining suspense. How about you?

Discovery is an integral part of every successful production for stage and screen. Actors, dancers, and vocalists must find what is compelling in their roles and recreate that magic, performance after performance. Actors often search deeply within themselves to find those experiences that can provide meaning for their particular characters. Any story often works best when the writer leaves much unsaid, when imagination is sparked, when minds are engaged and hearts touched.

Paradigm Shifts

Certainly, scholars in the future will disprove some of what everyone considers factual today. They will certainly modify much more. That's the nature of progress. New paradigms will inevitably emerge to rival the old (Kuhn 1970). What can you do to prepare your students for the changes that no one can now predict? What can you do for yourself?

Some shifts in thinking happen gradually. Others are dramatic. For example, controversy about human evolution began explosively when Charles Darwin published *Origins of the Species* and continues in one way or another today through debates about the teaching of creationism. *Survival of the fittest* is a concept that continues to crop up in various guises — for example, as social Darwinism to justify the capitalistic notion of a meritocracy.

Or consider the ongoing debates about the appropriate role of the military during times of peace. Can troops from the United Nations really stem violence where long-standing ethnic hatreds run deep? Knowing what to do about brutal conflicts in the Middle East, the Balkans, or Africa in the 1990s can try anyone's confidence. Does a strong national defense promote peace? Or is it more likely that weapons and troops will be used because they are available? Does the continued development of advanced weaponry affect the ways in which countries relate to each other? As the reigning superpower in the 1990s, should the U.S. play "world cop"? If so, who pays for it? Honesty and openness seem to generate more questions than answers.

Debates in agriculture also rage as advocates of organic approaches battle their more "scientific" counterparts who prefer the control possible through chemical fertilizers, herbicides, and pesticides. Into this debate now come archaeologists who also challenge "modern" ways by helping rural communities in the Andes reclaim unproductive lands. Where malnutrition and hunger are currently widespread, ancient methods, canals, and terraces seem to hold promise for producing lush crops once again in an area long barren. Can paradigms shift backwards as well? Can we reclaim the future by returning to proven practices from the past? Great fuel for engaging drama, no?

Or consider the literature about business effectiveness where Peters and Waterman (1982) and Peters and Austin (1985) seem to have "rediscovered" some very old truths. Modern companies are reminded of the necessity to stay "close to the knitting" and concentrate on what they do best, to "care for their customers," while they also innovate and push for new discoveries — which, in terms of their management practices, may indeed be very old ideas about the place for quality and common sense!

Meanwhile, technological advances and computers, in particular, add to the pressure on old paradigms, automating routine work, increasing access to information, and adding ever new and more powerful tools for data analysis. Teachers at all levels are also swept up into this shift. From desktop publishing to computer-mediated learning to distance education, we have new options for improving our teaching, better engaging students, and promoting deeper learning.

By using the performing paradigm to help incorporate the stories of discovery that form the history of every discipline, we believe that you can paint a more memorable picture of the advance of knowledge and exchange of ideas that underlie your courses. As students move into these fields, they can then draw on these lessons, both as content and process, for examples of what it takes to be a leader in a field.

A Place for Curiosity

Discovery is fueled by a human interest in the unknown. Curiosity is one of those qualities everyone possesses from birth, undoubtedly linked to survival. Yet some of the loudest critics of schooling — Ivan Illich, Jonathan Holt, Jonathan Kozol, A.S. Neill, Howard Gardner — have long decried the complicity of our educational system in the loss of curiosity among students. How can individual interest prevail, they have asked, when control is emphasized over curiosity, when correct form is more important than the substance of underlying thought processes, when learning is prescribed by experts, and when the use of computer-scored, multiple-choice tests emphasizes recall of information, what Freire termed the "banking" notion of education? Behavioral research seems very clear about the damage that is done to individual interests when extrinsic rewards dominate instruction.

In class, you may well accomplish much more by teaching less. Consider Joel Primack (Physics, University of California, Santa Cruz). In teaching introductory physics over the years, he has found discovery to be an important mechanism for correcting the myths and misconceptions that students bring to class. However, he has had little success in attacking these myths directly; when he does, his students only attempt to memorize some new "truth" without really changing their beliefs. Instead, Primack has found that discovery, and computer games in particular, allow students to experience the world anew and see firsthand that certain beliefs just do not hold up.

To illustrate this point, Primack uses a demonstration in class that involves motion and a dropped object. He poses a concrete situation — "If I run across the front of the class and release an eraser directly above a wastebasket, will the eraser (a) land in the wastebasket, (b) land on the floor past the basket, or (c) land at some other point?" Many students have an intuitive or common sense expectation that dropped objects move directly downward, regardless of any motion which precedes or contains the drop. Having polled his students, he performs the experiment. He can then probe their thinking and try to undo any misconceptions.

Approaches to Discovery

Two powerful engines of the discovery process are induction (hypothesis formation) and deduction (hypothesis testing). These basic approaches can add the "minds-on" factor that provides teachers with new possibilities for conveying — and exploring — ideas and information. Each has a role in capturing and channeling curiosity toward resolving unknowns. Each has a role in the development of productions for the stage and critical thinking for the classroom.

Think of the various races, debates, and controversies among scientists and scholars that dot the historical landscape of every field: James Watson and Francis Crick dueling to be the first to describe the nature of DNA; the critical reception that critics so often give new works of art, music, or dance, and how Igor Stravinsky was panned when *The Rites of Spring* was first performed; the recent controversy over cold fusion and what may have been premature claims; the current worldwide competition over cures for cancer and AIDS. Your own field doubtless offers some interesting stories of discovery. Can you use them to engage your students?

The Emotions of Discovery

While you can certainly use stories, puzzles, and problems to captivate and challenge, you may also need to support your students emotionally as they learn to deal with what is perplexing or unknown. If solutions are difficult or the process is long, students can become frustrated. They may tire and need help to stay enthused and on task. They may need the ongoing support and assistance of a small group of peers, a team. They will certainly need to see discovery valued somehow in your assessment system.

You can often use empathy to show that you understand their struggles. You can accept their struggles as part of the learning process and resist your impulse to run to their rescue too quickly. You can take a few minutes here and there to share your observations, to listen to their concerns. You can provide guidance, support, and encouragement for navigating discovery-based assignments as well as regular reminders about the history of ideas and the potential importance of these kinds of exercises. You can also teach them directly about paradigm shifts and the roles that human emotions have played in advancing or stifling breakthroughs.

Emotions are obviously critical to success on the stage, not only to develop believable characters but to provide the necessary energy for bringing a complex creative production to life. The challenge of it all can really bond a group of strangers into a tight cast and crew in a very short time. Part of this process reflects the demands of rehearsal, in which long hours are spent in focused study, experimentation, and refinement, intensified by feedback from directors, conductors, and choreographers. Part reflects the demands of a public performance, where no amount of sincere effort can guarantee audience approval.

Induction

Moving from the most rudimentary hunches and bits of data to a full-blown hypothesis that attempts to provide fundamental understanding is at the heart of much research. Using the inductive process in class means beginning with raw data or descriptive information. You can then guide students through a process to group this "stuff" and consider useful labels. Once they've reached some tentative agreements, you can lead a discussion about the potential interrelationships among these categories. Ultimately, you try to generate hypotheses with generalizable concepts. The drama here can derive from the active involvement of students in the construction of meaning. Instead of limiting them to the passive intake of information, you ask them actively to help organize data in ways that make sense to them and then to test out those ideas.

For example, scholars have identified a long list of teacher qualities that students consider effective. When Timpson teaches this material, he often uses an inductive approach to draw from students and generate a list based on their experiences. The drama evolves from the uncertainty of the process. Ultimately, he guides his students toward unspecified conclusions which he can then contrast with the published research on teacher effectiveness. Although this process takes time, it energizes and empowers students by grounding their understanding in the context of their own personal experiences.

As with discovery, some students may find induction frustrating and confusing. However, if you stress that the process is important to critical thinking, they can rise to the challenge. As with discovery, you can use empathy, acceptance, and reflective listening to help your students understand and manage their feelings effectively in support of deeper learning.

In the theatre and on film, you can see evidence of inductive thinking, especially where actors try to connect the actions of a character's
life into a believable whole that "hangs together." Directors play a
role similar to that of teachers, in reflecting back what they are seeing
in rehearsal and guiding their actors through this process.

Deduction

"It's elementary, Watson!" proclaimed Sherlock Holmes when
pressed to explain his reasoning. Once Holmes had pieced together
the threads of evidence to solve the knottiest of crimes, he would connect them all in a staggering display of intellect and deductive reasoning. Beginning with the underlying motivation, Holmes would string
together the critical events and explain all, down to seemingly irrelevant minutiae, which were, in fact, essential clues for unraveling the
mystery.

Every discipline has its Holmes types who know how to play regularly to students in the collective embodiment of a Watson. You too
can do much the same and add a bit of drama to your presentations,
carefully unfolding the details of various lines of research, for example, giving students insight into all those factors that affect the discovery process — the clues along the way, the blind alleys, the good
luck, the tedious work, the influence of other characters in the plot.

Case Studies and Problem-Based Learning

Using case studies, problem-based learning, and other student-centered approaches can give you many opportunities to mix discovery
with drama. You can always challenge students to be more active.

Case studies, for example, have been popular in business and law
schools for years. Several medical schools have adopted problems as a
central organizing focus for their curricula and classroom instruction.
One major benefit is the closer connection between what happens in
class and what is demanded in the field. The drama of the real world
can help you better engage and energize students.

As mentioned earlier, Marty Fettman makes extensive use of case
studies for teaching pathology in a veterinary school. This approach
allows Fettman to lead off with a real problem. In this way, he uses
class less for information transmission and more to set the stage for

inductive inquiry, describing symptoms and case histories, but then challenging students to dig through their texts and other sources for solutions, just like a practicing veterinarian. Unlike traditional approaches in which students are expected — often to little or no avail — to complete required readings before class and come prepared to participate, Fettman's students come to each new case without any specific preparation, equipped only with their experiences, knowledge, and thinking abilities. Cases then evolve rapidly, with Fettman playing the interrogator: "What would you see under the microscope? Give me another example. Give me the pathway. What about ...? What would be the point of ...? What would happen if ...? What are the principle muscles at work here? Did everybody follow that?"

The case study approach puts an emphasis on modeling the processes that professionals in the field use to address real issues and problems. Students move from the position of novices who lack the necessary background to roles as active participants in high-level analysis and problem resolution who learn what they need along the way. The process of learning becomes as important as the knowledge itself.

In this pathology class, drama became important in several ways: first, in framing a case and its importance through an animal with a particular set of symptoms; second, in surfacing opinions about the pathology involved and how each could be assessed; third, in whatever discussion or debate ensued; and fourth, in the ultimate resolution after completing all the analyses and research.

The drama here can be very real. You can challenge students to think, to analyze, to seek out additional information and come to class prepared to present or defend their arguments. You can play the devil's advocate and raise alternative views. This can also be great fun for everyone, as the methodical, information-driven lecture approach gives way to a highly interactive, dynamic forum.

Another example using case studies, from a different discipline, may help clarify some of these connections between discovery and drama. Wally Bacon (Political Science, University of Nebraska at Omaha) frames his International Relations class as an extended role-play exercise. He divides the class of 40-60 first- and second-year students into groups of three or four. Each group represents a country. Within the "countries," each group member assumes the role of specialist in a particular area: economics, internal security, foreign policy, or intelligence. As G.O.D. (Game Overall Director), Bacon creates a situation and a context, such as an international conference, which require each group of students to make decisions regarding how their country will interact with other countries. The goal for each team is to maximize what its country gets out of the negotiations.

One of Bacon's instructional objectives is to give students experience in doing library research and handling information. Here again, the performance aspect of the assignment helps to motivate students. They must research their "characters" extensively. Each group needs to learn not only about its own country (since they can't depart radically from a country's policy as it exists) but about the other countries. Bacon requires each country to put out a weekly news bulletin, which may be propagandistic. Other countries have to figure out how accurate the "news" is.

Providing a cooperative learning experience is another objective for the course. Each group has to come up with its own system for making decisions. Collaboratively, they use the information they've found through their research — and the textbook readings on theory — in developing a strategy or policy profile that will maximize their country's achievements. The process challenges students in that they have to defend orally in class positions with which they personally may disagree.

After this process, the students engage in a thorough written assessment. Again, they apply the theories they've been learning as they critique themselves and the other teams. To a large extent, Bacon depends on the students' assessments to determine grades.

His overriding objective (or "spine") for the course is to empower students to think independently. He believes that they learn more through applying theory in the role-play than they would by studying pure theory in an ordinary lecture/discussion format.

Concluding Thoughts

As with the case we made for drama and development, here again we find the performance paradigm enormously helpful for teachers who want to use inductive and other discovery-based approaches. There is much research evidence linking higher levels of motivation with inquiry. Teachers who use discovery and some of the performer's skills and practices can better energize and engage their students. Again, we say, "Go for it!"

Chapter 10
Performance-Enhancing Exercises

Performers routinely use exercises to explore new possibilities, expand their ranges, and hone their skills. Whether to explore some new idea or play with improvisation, whether to perfect certain movements or develop greater vocal range, exercises can prove stimulating, useful, and fun. In this chapter we offer some activities for you to consider. If you want support and a social context, invite colleagues to join in.

Many beginning acting exercises serve two functions: to help individuals explore various aspects of performance an, to build a supportive group dynamic. Such exercises usually involve the whole group, with everyone exploring simultaneously; no one is put on the spot to "perform" for others, except, perhaps, for a moment here or there.

Getting Started

Most performance training takes place in a group setting. Acting involves interacting — with others and/or the environment. If you want to improve your performance skills for teaching, we encourage you to form a support group of teachers willing to devote some time to exploring the benefits of performance-based exercises. Some acting exercises you can do on your own, but many require at least two participants and an audience. A support group can also provide feedback to group members and — very important — encouragement and assistance for forays into new territory.

Acting teachers devote the first few class periods of any course to developing an atmosphere in which students feel safe and supported by both the teacher and fellow students. All participants must believe they can take risks. Success on stage requires vulnerability, as actors explore new ways of experiencing and behaving, as they confront their inhibitions and fears.

If we teachers say we want to improve our performance skills, we are really saying we want to change our teaching behavior. While change can be scary, it can also be exhilarating, rewarding, and renewing. One of the reasons why many acting teachers subscribe to Spolin's "game" approach to training is that games can help make learning fun, help participants overcome their inhibitions, and liberate creative energy.

The "setting" you choose can support or inhibit the climate for change. It's good to have the use of a large, open space, preferably carpeted, with a few chairs and a table to use as "scenery" for improvisations. This space should be secure from interruptions, so participants feel more comfortable about entering into the exercises. Some soundproofing helps, not only to lessen distracting noises from the outside but also to reduce the chances that any noises you make will disturb others. "Lighting" can also affect the mood of a group. In contrast to harsh or fluorescent light, natural or soft, mellow lighting can create a mood more conducive to learning — a concept apparently missed by those who design most campus classrooms.

We recommend that your support group spend time during your first meetings establishing "ground rules" and developing trust. One way to start would be for members of the group to share their reasons for wanting to participate, their experience with performance work, their fears about acting, and their perceptions of their strengths and weaknesses as teachers.

We have already mentioned our own use of "trust exercises" for teaching — where students take turns closing their eyes and falling into the arms of group members or where one student leads a blindfolded partner around the room — to underscore learning to trust and to promote group support for risk-taking in class. While we offer a wide range of exercises throughout this book, we also encourage you to explore acting texts for other ideas and exercises. We particularly recommend Spolin's *Improvisation for the Theater* and Boal's *Games for Actors and Non-Actors*.

The first two chapters of *Improvisation for the Theater* provide a good introduction to the theory of developing creative behavior as well as a useful guide to ground rules for a workshop. Spolin emphasizes that performance training is by nature experiential learning — we learn by doing and we learn in the process of doing. Value judgments about what we should be doing can activate our inhibitions and limit the potential impact of any experience. Using exercises and games can help us open up to new possibilities without distracting preconceptions.

With its orientation toward industrial development, technology, and market forces, Western culture tends to reinforce a kind of competitive thinking that puts a premium on winning the approval of customers, investors, government leaders, and others. However, such dependency on the judgment of others can limit our learning as individuals. For example, there is no single "right" way to play Hamlet; every actor brings something unique to the role. The format for an acting exercise, therefore, involves establishing the "rules of the game," experiencing the activity, and then sharing our reactions and learning — as participants and/or as observers.

Approaching the exercises as problems to be solved also helps to keep a focus on the activity itself and away from any inhibiting need for approval. Discussing whether a group member found a solution to a problem is easier (thus less inhibiting) than making a value judgment about whether that person is a "good" or "bad" performer.

Nor should we expect to find the "perfect" solution to a performance problem the first time — or even the second or third time — we try an exercise. Like other skills, performance skills develop with practice. As we struggle with a challenging exercise, we can expect periods of frustration to be balanced by the joy of "breakthrough" and moments of insight.

Warm-Ups

Throughout this book, we have argued for the value of warm-ups. Indeed, we have devoted a chapter to them. In a workshop setting, warm-ups help participants clear their minds of distractions, limber up bodies and voices, and build group trust. Stretches, arm swings, head and trunk rotations, humming, singing — whatever works to relieve your tensions, loosen your muscles, and focus your energies. The members should take turns leading warm-ups. If you feel any anxiety about the public nature of this kind of activity, just remind yourself that you and your fellow group members have granted yourselves artistic license to be weird ... or anything else for that matter. It may also help to remember that what you're doing is for your students.

A warm-up routine can also become a kind of ritual that marks a transition from everyday life into a secure space and time for your group to work and play. For example, standing in a circle and massaging each other's shoulders can help everyone relax and focus. Look through the exercises we recommend here for ways to get started. Acting texts provide additional sources for these kinds of exercises.

We like to begin with some general exercises, then move to vocal and physical warm-ups. To awaken sense-awareness and spontaneity, we also offer a few theatre games here, then suggest some exercises more specifically aimed at developing performance skills for teachers. As you explore these exercises, you may also find some that you can adapt for use in class.

Beginning Exercises and Ground Rules

One group member serves as "guide" for each exercise, explaining the "rules of the game," guiding the other members, and leading the discussion afterwards. Guides help create a supportive atmosphere. They encourage everyone to explore. They also watch for flagging energies or interests, when they might suggest ending one game and moving on to something else.

Obviously, experience will help here. If you are new to the guide's role, just think of it as a volunteer leader who explains the rules, observes the process, and provides feedback when the activity is over. There is no formula, however. We recommend that guides periodically solicit feedback about their role and recommendations from the group for improvement.

When "processing" the game in the follow-up discussion, the guide encourages all members to share their experiences, no matter what that experience may be. Remember: there are no "right" or "wrong" reactions. Different people will have different experiences. For instance, when playing games that explore sensory awareness and imagination, you should keep in mind that different people favor different sensory/imaginative modes — visual, aural, kinesthetic, etc. When asked to imagine something, you may report visual images, for example, while someone else reports tactile sensations.

People can also have different emotional responses to an exercise. For example, most people enjoy a relaxation exercise in which they are asked to imagine themselves lying on a beach. Those who don't like heat or associate beaches with some unpleasant personal experience, however, may react negatively. One important rule is the "right of egress" — that is, group members must feel free at any time to withdraw from an exercise if they become uncomfortable.

If a group member chooses to withdraw during a game, the guide should later unobtrusively check in with that person to make sure everything is all right. After the exercise, perhaps during "processing," the person may want to explain his or her reaction; there should be no pressure to do so, however, if the group is to sustain its commitment to trust.

Especially during early sessions, group members may report feeling silly or self-conscious. Some may report being unable to stay focused on the exercise, for example, to imagine they were walking through Jell-O™ (or whatever a particular exercise required). During the time set aside for "processing," the guide encourages group members to share their reactions, including negative ones, and to understand that any experience is valid. Open and honest communication is essential.

Processing an exercise can also include some discussion about possible implications for teaching. The guide can ask group members to share their insights here. Throughout this book, we have made numerous comparisons between performance on stage and in class. Closing each processing session with a discussion of professional applications keeps the group members grounded in their reason for doing these exercises: to teach more effectively and help their students learn better.

Performance-Based Exercises

The following exercises can help you become more aware of your skills and point toward areas for improvement. Try a few. Remember that these are like calisthenics: they get you to stretch your creative abilities and explore new possibilities. They really have little in common otherwise. These exercises should be fun, and they should energize and inspire your teaching.

Woodchuck

Remember the old tongue-twister, "How much wood could a woodchuck chuck if a woodchuck could chuck wood?" To play this game, ask the group members to stand in a circle. Each will in turn say one word of the tongue-twister. The game puts a few "twists" on the old twister, though. You divide "woodchuck" into two words, "wood" and "chuck." Conversely, "could a" and "if a" become single words ("coulda" and "ifa" — shh, don't tell the English profs!). Thus the sentence becomes "How much wood coulda wood chuck chuck ifa wood chuck could chuck wood?" Explain the changes and have the group repeat the new version two or three times.

Part 1
Start the sentence moving around the circle. Each person gives his/her word to the person on his/her right, looking directly in the person's eyes. That person then gives the next word in the sentence to the person on his/her right, and so on around the circle. The person who "receives" the last word in the sentence starts over with the first word of the sentence, giving that word to the person on his/her right. As the sentence continues to move around the circle, coach the group to speed it up, giving the words as quickly as possible.

Part 2
After the group has become skilled at passing the words, explain Part 2. In this variation, members give the word by pointing at any other member in the circle. That person must quickly give the next word, pointing at someone else, and so on. Again, coach the group to keep the sentence moving as quickly as possible.

Variation #1
In one variation of Part 2, "Shoot-out at the OK Corral," anyone who says the wrong word or fails to keep the sentence moving at the group's quick pace has been "shot" and drops out of the game. The game continues until there is a winner — the last cowpoke left alive.

Variation #2

In another variation, players add emotions to the words, responding to the emotional tonality given to the word passed by the previous player. For instance, one player might shout angrily, "HOW!" The second player might respond, "much," in a hurt tone. The third might say, "wood," in a comforting tone. And so on around the circle. Again, insist that the sentence keep moving quickly.

Processing

Questions to consider:

- What did you experience?

- What particular "problems" does the exercise pose? Did you solve the problems? If so, how?

- What skills does the exercise develop? Why do actors need these skills? Teachers?

- Could this exercise be a good ice-breaker for students, building team spirit for a group activity or project?

- Does a lively class discussion or debate ever move this fast and really require you to be on your toes?

This simple game certainly promotes concentration and group awareness. And, it's fun. Anyone who stops listening for even a moment will be lost. Actors need intense concentration to stay "in the moment" on stage in order to create a convincing stage reality. Genuine listening and staying "in the moment" can help teachers respond better to the dynamics in their classes. Actors doing the woodchuck game often observe that this kind of exercise helps them learn to "pick up their cues," to keep the pace of a scene moving. Pace is certainly an issue for teachers. For example, students who seem bored may be frustrated with a slow and deliberate pace that never varies. Greater awareness of pace could make you more alert to needed changes and variety.

This exercise also develops spontaneity. Part 2 require players to make choices. As the pace picks up, players no longer have time to think about their choices; they must react with their first impulse. Variation #2 requires players to "read" emotional tonality and to respond intuitively. Certainly there will be times in class when you need to be more spontaneous, when students are stuck or restless, when you must use your intuition to come up with a different explanation or an alternative activity.

Adverb Game

Designate one member to be "it." "It" goes out of the room and the other members agree upon an adverb (e.g., "resentfully," "slowly," "frantically," "clumsily," etc.).

After returning, "it" asks somebody to perform a simple action: walk across the room, greet another member, or stand on a chair, for instance. That person must perform the action in the manner of the chosen adverb. "It" must guess the adverb; the other members must communicate to "it" the adverb through their manner of performing the actions.

If "it" cannot guess the adverb from the first performer's action, he or she continues to ask other members to carry out simple actions until the adverb becomes clear. The others also give clues through their collective behavior. From the time "it" returns to the room, the others suggest the adverb in the way they sit, talk, etc.

After "it" guesses the adverb, the group selects a new "it" and a new adverb and repeats the game. One important rule: no group member can say the adverb or a variant of the adverb while "it" is in the room.

Processing
Questions to consider:

- What did you experience?

- What particular problems does the exercise pose? Did you solve the problems? If so, how?

- What skills does the exercise develop? Why do actors need these skills? Teachers?

- Do students give nonverbal clues that can allow you insights into their reactions?

- What clues do you give about your interest in your material, your students, and your teaching?

The adverb game allows experimentation with expressive behavior in performing simple tasks. The group setting enhances trust and reduces performance anxiety. This is a "win/win" type of game, with both "it" and the other members focused on the same goal: successful communication through nonverbal means. As members become more skilled at the game, they may choose more difficult adverbs to enact.

Foreign language teachers may wish to experiment with the adverb game as a tool to add life and energy to vocabulary building. The game can easily be adapted so that "it" gives instructions in the target language — and seeks to identify an adverb chosen from that language.

Any teacher who uses group learning for projects or presentations might find value in this game for helping students sharpen their awareness of the emotional components that underlie team success.

Rhythmic Sound and Movement

Because most teachers are so dependent on language, exercises that involve movements, gestures, and other kinds of sounds can be challenging, developing awareness about all the factors that influence communications, teaching, and learning.

Part 1
The members form a circle, with one person in the middle. The one in the middle (leader) performs a rhythmic movement accompanied by a sound — no words allowed. The stranger the pattern and the more it involves voice and body, the better. The leader repeats the pattern and everyone in the circle imitates the pattern of sound and movement as exactly as possible. The leader then changes places with one of the players in the circle, who moves into the center to become the new leader. The exercise continues until everyone has had the opportunity to lead.

Part 2
Play this variation the same way as Part 1, except that the leader must perform a rhythmic sound and movement that expresses how he or she is feeling that day.

Part 3
You can also have the group string all the sounds and movements together, repeating each person's contribution as it is introduced and then periodically reviewing each one, from first to last. Once everyone has introduced something, you can then "pass the action around" by having individuals repeat what someone else has offered. Then, to keep the action moving, whoever originally introduced that sound and movement must repeat someone else's.

Processing

Questions to consider:

- What did you experience?

- What particular problems does the exercise pose? Did you solve the problems? If so, how?

- Was your experience of Parts 2 or 3 different from your experience of Part 1? If so, how?

- What skills does the exercise develop? Why do actors need these skills? Teachers?

- Could this kind of activity help students develop empathy and sensitivity toward others? How?

Boal uses a version of Part 1 in his workshops and stresses the significance of imitating the leader's patterns as exactly as possible; for instance, if a woman leads, the men in the circle must try not to produce a "masculine" version of the pattern. Boal (1992, 89) points out that this exercise provides a step toward change, allowing you to explore your own potential by trying out very different responses.

> What is happening here? What mechanism is at play? In the act of trying to reproduce someone else's way of moving, singing, etc., we begin to undo our own *mechanizations* and raise our consciousness about possible change. When we are responding to the lead of others, we are trying on their ideas. We are stretching, exploring, experimenting, and — ultimately — rethinking our own ways of behaving.

> We do not do a caricature, because that would lead us to do different things but in our own way. We try to understand and make an exact copy of the exterior of the person in the middle, in order to gain a better understanding of his or her interior.

Part 2 serves an additional function, requiring the leader to focus on his or her immediate feelings and to express those feelings physically and vocally. In processing, players often comment on the cathartic value of the experience. If the day has been upsetting or frustrating, venting those feelings can help a player let go of them and focus better on the present. For this reason, your group might wish to incorporate this exercise into your warm-up ritual. As a warm-up, it also provides a quick means of "checking in" on everybody's mood as the session begins.

Space Walk

Part 1

The guide asks the other members to begin walking through the space in the room, explaining that he or she will give instructions as the exercise proceeds and emphasizing that this is a personal exploration, not an interactive game.

The guide first asks the others to explore the space through which they are moving as if it were a new substance. How does it feel to walk through this space?

Then the guide explains that he or she will call out different substances — warm water, gritty mud, cobwebs, cotton candy, orange Jell-O™, champagne, anything weird or wonderful — and ask the members to imagine that they are moving through each. The guide coaches the players, "Imagine that all of the space in the room has transformed into the new substance — but all of you can still breathe!"

Finally, the guide instructs the players to return to reality and explore the space in the room again as it is. How does this contrast with moving through the other substances?

Processing

Questions to consider:

- What did you experience?

- What particular problems does the exercise pose? Did you solve the problems? If so, how?

- Were some substances easier to imagine than others? Why?

- What skills does the exercise develop? Why do actors need these skills? Teachers?

- Could this exercise help you become more aware of the disjunction that may occur between your message and your gestures, nonverbal expressions, or movements in class?

Part 1 of the exercise deals with sensory awareness and imagination. Players often report difficulty in imagining themselves moving through unusual substances. After all, when do we ever walk through Jell-O™? As we describe in our chapter on creativity, however, imaginative abilities are like other skills and can be developed with practice. Developing more creative approaches to teaching and learning could energize you and your students and counteract the deadening effect of routine. In *Improvisation for the Theater*, Spolin devotes considerable time in beginning sessions to imagination and sensory awareness exercises.

Part 2

Note: This activity may be more challenging for new guides, but the benefits for players can make it worthwhile with even the most inexperienced guide.

Divide the group in half. One half will perform the exercise while the other half observes. The guide again asks the players to walk through the space in the room, calling out additional instructions as the activity unfolds. Here, the guide and the observers examine the players closely, noting in which parts of the body individuals seem to carry most of their tension. During the ensuing exercise, the guide can try to emphasize those parts of the body.

First, the guide coaches the players to allow the space to support them: "Let this space support your head, your shoulders, your forehead, your knees," etc. As the players move, the guide continues to coach that the space supports them.

The guide then announces to the players that space no longer supports them; they must do something or they will fly into a million, billion pieces: "Grab your shoulders. Hold onto your eyeballs, your chin, your neck, your fingers," etc.

Then the guide returns the activity to the beginning by telling the players that space is supporting them again. The guide continues to alternate between space support and lack of support until players clearly experience the difference between the two.

Repeat the exercise, with the observers becoming the players and the first group of players now observing.

Processing
Questions to consider:

- Ask the players what they experienced when space supported them. What was the difference when they had to support themselves?

- Ask the observers what differences they noted.

- How does your teaching space support you — physically, intellectually, emotionally? How does it limit you?

- Have you given yourself permission to explore what could be possible? Or do you let your preconceptions narrow your options? Does the design of the lecture hall inhibit you from walking up and down the aisles to facilitate discussions? Can you reframe that teacher/student barrier at the front and incorporate more student presentations? What other alternatives are possible? Can you go outside? Are field trips possible?

Spolin (1983, 82) observes that this exercise can help participants become aware of which parts of their own bodies they habitually hold rigid. She notes, "One student who customarily had a tight expression on his face that gave him what might be called a 'mean' look first became aware of his rigidity through this exercise." Certainly a valuable discovery for teachers!

Acting requires performers to study themselves, to become aware of personal habits. To transform themselves into characters, actors must identify their own habits and patterns, so they can change them as needed. Likewise, teachers wishing to improve their teaching need to analyze their personal patterns and make choices about what to keep and what to change.

Part 3

The guide again divides the group into players and observers and asks players to walk through the space in that room. This time, when the guide calls out different parts of the body, the players are to imagine that part as the "center" that initiates movement. Players may find it helpful to imagine a string attached to that part of the body, pulling them through the space. The guide thus calls out, for instance: "Nose, left shoulder, right knee, chin, breastbone, pelvis, right ear, left big toe, navel," etc., each time giving players sufficient time to experience the new "center."

Then the guide instructs the players to move "normally" through space. As they do so, the guide coaches them to try to identify what serves as their own habitual center of movement.

Repeat the exercise, reversing players and observers.

Processing

Questions to consider:

- Ask the players how they experienced the different centers.

- Ask the observers what the players looked like when moving and when being pulled, for example, from the nose.

- Were players able to identify their own habitual centers? If not, you could assign everyone a partner and ask the partners to observe each other's movement and help to identify the center.

- Would there be times in teaching when you could change your posture or movements to emphasize a point or show empathy, for example, when students are anxious about an upcoming exam, forgetful about assignments, or struggling with a problem?

One "outside-in" approach to playing a role has to do with selecting an appropriate center for the character and developing a posture and movement pattern based on that center. An obvious choice of center for a gossipy, inquisitive character, for example, might be the nose! Benedetti (1976, 79) argues that there are "five primary character centers that, by bodily logic and by cultural tradition, are each associated with a different sort of person." He encourages acting students to study these character types in order to make choices about where to place their character's center.

In order to be able to make choices about character centers, however, actors work to develop a "neutral" postural alignment and to strengthen their sense of how energy and movement flow from their own personal center. This "centering" work enhances the actor's "stage presence." Stage presence can also be useful in teaching. Your ability to sense the need for a change can help keep students engaged. Your ability to monitor the time you have available in class can ensure appropriate pacing and allow for adequate summaries, processing, or reminders about upcoming requirements. The following exercise explores energy and centering.

Energy Center

The guide will coach the players through all parts of the exercise, allowing sufficient time to explore each activity before explaining the next. *Note:* There should be no verbal interaction among players during this exercise.

Part 1 — Finding Center

Begin with the "Hanging Yourself Up" exercise explained in the chapter on warm-ups. Then explore your center in the following stages:

- Move either foot to the side about two feet; rock from foot to foot, feeling your center of gravity moving from side to side. Gradually come to rest on center like a pendulum.

- Move either foot forward about two feet; find your center with front-to-back motions.

- Rotate your center around, exploring the limits of various stances. Feel the weight of your body flowing into the ground out of your center through your legs; feel "rooted," as if your weight were a root reaching into the ground beneath you.

- Bring your feet together and explore the center.

- Imagine a cord entering the top of the head and attached to your center. "Lift" yourself upward in small jumps by "tugging" on this cord.

- Jump to a specific place by lifting the center, then putting it down on your destination. You land perfectly centered, stable and without jiggling, but lightly. At no time in your jump do you lose your center.

- Walk to a specific place by lifting the center up through the top of your head, holding it up while you walk, and setting it down at your destination.

Part 2 — The Energy Center

The guide gives the following instructions.

- Hang yourself up once again. Stand with legs comfortably apart, knees slightly flexed (not locked). Find your center.

- Now focus on your breathing. Breathe deeply, comfortably, and naturally. Imagine an energy center in the middle of your body. You may visualize this center however you wish. You might imagine it, for example, as a little glowing sun. Imagine that with each breath you take, you bring energy in from the outside world and store it in your center — the center glows more brightly. Continue to breathe deeply, storing energy in your center and enjoying the glowing warmth in the center of your body.

- As you continue to breathe, imagine that energy is flowing from your center down through your legs, through your ankles and feet, making contact with the earth. Don't worry if you don't "really" feel the energy flowing in this exercise. Imagine that you do; imagine what it would be like to feel the flow of energy. Feel and enjoy the flow of energy from your center, down through your legs, down through your feet, grounding you.

- Now imagine energy flowing from your center up through your chest, into your shoulders, down through your arms, into your hands, out the palms of your hands and your fingertips, making contact with the air. Enjoy the feeling of the energy flowing through your upper body and arms. You may even feel a slight tingle in your fingers as the energy flows through them.

- Again, imagine energy flowing from your center up through your chest. This time, the energy continues up your neck, into your head, flowing out your eyes and the top of your head, making contact with the air.

- As you continue to breathe, deeply, easily, you store more energy in your center, which glows brighter and brighter. This energy continues to flow — down your legs, through your feet, into the earth. Up through your chest, down your arms, out your hands and fingertips. Up through your chest, through your neck, into your head, out your eyes and the top of your head.

Part 3 — Attract/Reject

The guide then asks players to begin to move throughout the room, remaining aware of the energy flowing from their centers and throughout their bodies as they move. After allowing players to experience movement with energy flow, the guide announces that he or she will call out, in turn, three different uses of the energy: attract, reject, and neutral. On the cue, "Attract," the players should use their energy to "attract," to "pull" the other players toward them. (*Note:* Players may feel more comfortable if the guide instructs them that the "attractive" use of energy need not be sexual in nature.) On the cue,

"Reject," players use their energy to "reject," to "push" the other players away from them. On "Neutral," players remain aware of the energy flow and of the other players but neither attract nor reject with their energy. In all three cases, players should continue to move through the room and to make eye contact with other players as they move past them.

Processing
Questions to consider:

- What did you experience?

- What particular problems does the exercise pose? Did you solve the problems? If so, how?

- Did you feel most comfortable using energy to attract, to reject, or in neutral?

- What skills does the exercise develop? Why do actors need these skills? Teachers?

- When might your movements add some fun energy to a discussion of the attractions and rejections that occur in nature, with magnets, sub-atomic particles, chemicals, personalities, or ideas?

Some people seem most comfortable using energy to attract — to mobilize resources and lead or to socialize with others and work in teams. Others can be abrasive, perhaps focusing more on goals and outcomes, and thus push people away with their energy. Certainly, there are situations when using "rejective" energy is appropriate or when you may wish to "hide" with neutral energy, not wanting to draw attention to yourself.

You yourself may use energy in these ways without being aware when you are doing so. Encourage group members to pay attention to their use of energy during the following week, especially in class, and note moments when they become aware of using energy to attract or reject.

As you become more aware of energy, you may begin to notice more about your students and their energy, such as how the push and pull of individual energies can affect small group activities. Indeed, this exercise may prove valuable for your students to experience if you assign group work.

Since energy flow and stage presence can be heightened through centering and conscious awareness of energy use, group members could incorporate parts of this exercise into their personal pre-class warm-up routines. The group may also benefit from repeating the exercise at future sessions, to practice "attracting" and "rejecting" each other. You can incorporate energy awareness into other exercises, such as the "mirroring" exercise described elsewhere in this book.

More Advanced Work

When you feel comfortable with these introductory exercises, you may want to explore others that are more challenging. As you consider these, monitor your level of comfort. What inhibitions do you feel? The more you can become aware of these blocks, the more you will be free to grow in new directions. Above all, have fun! Create. Explore possibilities in yourself and with others. The benefits for your teaching will evolve as you grow more aware of yourself and others.

Inner Monologue

Actors who work "inside-out" use a technique called "inner monologue." To experience the power of inner monologue, do the following exercise with your group.

A sidewalk serves as the setting for the improvisation. Two people play the scene. Starting from opposite sides of the room, each character will walk down an imaginary sidewalk, greet the other character, and then continue on his or her way. Each character has one line of dialogue. Character A will speak first and say, "Hello. How are you?" Character B will reply, "I'm fine. How are you?" The performers must say only the lines assigned to them, nothing else.

To prepare for this exercise, write on slips of paper a line or two of "inner monologue" — in other words, what one of the characters might be thinking while greeting the other. Examples:

- "I'll never forgive you for what you did to me!"

- "What's happened to you? You look awful!"

- "What have I done to offend you?"

- "No time to talk! I'm late for an important meeting."

- "The last time I saw you, I made a real fool of myself at that party. I hope you don't remember!"

- "I can't believe it! I just won the lottery!"

Put the slips of paper in an envelope.

Choose two members to play the scene and ask each player to draw a slip from the envelope. Instruct each player to think the inner monologue written on the paper while greeting the other character. Ask the rest of the group to observe the scene closely to see if they can identify what each character is thinking.

After each scene, ask the observers what the characters might have been thinking — and what the actor did that gave that impression. Then have the actors tell the group what thoughts they found on their slips of paper. Thank them for their "performance" and lead a round of applause.

Repeat the scene with two more players, who draw new slips of paper out of the envelope. Follow this "performance" with an analysis, as above. Repeat this exercise again until everyone has had a chance to "perform."

Processing
Questions to consider:

- As an actor, what did you experience?

- As an observer, could you tell what the performers were thinking? If so, how?

- What skills does the exercise develop? Why do actors need these skills? Teachers?

- When does your inner monologue color your words in class? When does your preoccupation with other work show through? Your tiredness? Your boredom with the material? Your frustration with unprepared, unresponsive, or rude students?

When analyzing the characters' thoughts, observers find clues in the players' nonverbal behavior: movement patterns, gestures, facial expressions, tone of voice. Someone might conclude, for instance, that a character was thinking aggressive thoughts because "Paul stood right in Sheila's path and glared at her. His voice seemed low and threatening."

Even when watching non-trained performers, the observers make interpretations that often correspond very closely with the assigned inner monologue. Why? For one thing, as part of our socialization process, we humans have learned to "read" nonverbal cues. For another, just thinking certain thoughts can influence your nonverbal behavior; you don't have to consciously design a behavior pattern.

Note that all of the pairs of characters who performed the exercise spoke the same words — yet the scenes as performed will look very different because of the emotional content and the relationships between the characters. Actors know very well that they cannot rely on words alone — the written dialogue — to communicate the emotional dynamics of a scene. "Inside-out" actors work to discover the "inner monologue" for their characters at every moment during the play. When performing, they actually think the character's thoughts, knowing that their voices and bodies will communicate those thoughts to an audience.

Students will be constantly reading your nonverbal cues. Reminding yourself of that fact may help you to make conscious choices about your "inner monologue." You may not be able to see yourself, but you can become more aware of what you are thinking and, thus, what nonverbal messages you may be sending.

While lecturing, are you thinking, "This is a really exciting insight!"? Or rather, "I really need to hurry to get through all this material"? When a student asks a question, if your inner monologue says, "Hey, I covered that last week!" then the student may pick up on your impatience, no matter how politely you word your response.

Communication is a two-way street, of course. As we've pointed out elsewhere in this book, actors on stage learn how to "read" an audience, making subtle changes to adjust to what they sense. If you can remember to keep checking the nonverbal responses of your students, you also can develop your abilities to pick up cues that can indicate when they are interested, confused, or just plain bored. Do you ever notice the glazed look in the eyes of a whole class at the end of a long and complicated explanation?

Objectives

Teachers often talk about instructional objectives — what they want the students to be able to do in measurable terms, for example, on papers, projects, or exams. Thinking this through and informing your students can really help keep your expectations clear and focused. In the theatre, action on stage is intensified when actors have competing objectives, when they want different things. Although the use of theatrical objectives is somewhat different from the use of instructional objectives, it's useful for teachers to explore.

For example, a performer trained in the Stanislavski system identifies his or her character's objectives for the play as a whole, for each individual scene, and for each part of a scene during which the objective remains unchanged. Actors will state their objectives as infinitive verb phrases. Why verbs? Because verbs are action words, thus easier to portray.

With your support group, try the following exercise in working with objectives.

Setting: A professor's office. You need a desk or table and two chairs.

Characters: A teacher and one of his or her students.

Situation: The student has missed an important exam for the teacher's class.

General objectives: The student just overslept, but wants to persuade the teacher to give him or her a make-up exam. Working with large classes and the frequent appeals from students for exceptions for this and that, the teacher has developed course policies that work well. Not believing that the student has a valid reason and thinking that the student needs to suffer the consequences, the teacher wants to refuse to give a make-up test.

In this first scene, we are setting up a "win-lose" situation. If you find this uncomfortable, rest assured that we will give you a chance to work with a "win-win" solution in Part 3.

Part 1
Ask for two volunteers, one to play the student and one to play the teacher. They will improvise the scene, each concentrating on trying to achieve his or her objective: the student will "win" if the teacher agrees to give a make-up exam and the teacher will "win" if the student gives up and leaves the office. If the improv goes on for more than three minutes and neither has "won," stop it and proceed to Part 2.

Part 2
Prior to the exercise, write on slips of paper infinitives that describe specific tactics that either the student or the teacher might use in order to achieve his or her objective. Some student tactics might be: to impress, to flatter, to threaten, to blame, to beg, to bargain, to charm.

Some teacher tactics might be: to ignore, to pass the buck, to justify, to ridicule, to psychoanalyze, to sympathize, to apologize. Put the "student" tactics in an envelope marked "student" and the "teacher" tactics in an envelope marked "teacher."

Repeat the improv, using the same actors, the same situation, and the same general objectives. This time, ask each actor to draw a tactic out of the appropriate envelope and to concentrate on playing that tactic, using it to achieve his or her objective. Ask the group to observe the improv closely to see if they can identify which tactics the players are using. Again, if the improv goes on for more than about three minutes without either player "winning," stop it, give the players a round of applause, and move into Part 3.

Part 3

Have these same actors now try to find a solution that is mutually agreeable and accommodates the needs of both parties as well as the course or institutional requirements.

Processing

Questions to consider:

- Ask the observers what tactics each character used. How could they tell?

- Which scene was more interesting to watch — the first, the second, or the third? Which was the best solution?

- Ask the actors which scene they thought easier to play. Why?

In most cases, the audience finds the second of the first two scenes livelier and more interesting. The players, too, usually discover the second version easier to play. The third scene may prove easiest of all, although clearly lacking in "dramatic content." Focusing on a specific, clearly stated tactic energizes the actor: he or she has something definite to do. Actors quickly realize that finding something to do on stage also relieves performance anxiety and self-consciousness.

Having clear objectives in mind for a class tends to provide appropriate energy, organization, and focus. Watching your use of the time available in class may give you clues about your real objectives. For example, if you have a "soft" start to class, you may value a more informal and relaxed climate that promotes easy and open interactions with students. If you have a more "driven" start, you may have a lot to cover and little time left for unplanned activity (including questions, comments, spontaneous debates, etc.).

Repeat Part 2 of the exercise, having each set of players draw new objectives (infinitives) from the envelopes, until everyone has had the opportunity to try the improv. Each time, applaud the players and ask the group what objectives the characters played.

Drawing from Boal's work with "Forum Theater," you could experiment with yet another approach to this scene. Start with the student as "protagonist" facing a seemingly impossible "antagonist." Other members of the group can say, "Stop!" at any point in the scene when they believe they have a new idea. That person then replaces the protagonist and the scene is replayed. After each scene, hold a brief discussion to attempt to analyze what new element was added, what new possibility was suggested. The scene is replayed again, proceeding until someone else has something new to offer.

Along the way, you want to keep asking, "Is this scene real?" Throughout the process, Boal insists on excluding "magical" solutions. The scene must stay grounded in a difficult and real context. In the end, everyone has contributed to a rethinking and replaying that is intended to provide for new possibilities.

Additional Processing
Questions to consider:

- Did the players solve the problem in the first two parts? Was there a point in any of the scenes at which one character spontaneously changed tactics? If so, why did this occur?

- How did the "win-win" scene differ from the "win-lose" scenes? From Boal's approach? Which scene was more real? More desirable?

Actors choose verbs for objectives that both specify the tactic used by their character to get what he or she wants from someone else and engage the actors' body and imagination. Effective objectives, in other words, stimulate the actor to action. Like the actor, you can also study your "scripts," your lesson plans, to identify the specific tactics that may most help you achieve your instructional goals for a class. Like the actor, you may wish to note in your lecture "script" a particular tactic-verb (objective) for each section of class. (Actors call these divisions "motivational units.")

For example, how can you use the concept of infinitive objectives inside and outside class? What happens when you focus less on coverage and more on what students are learning? What happens when you focus less on your explanations and more on what meaning students can construct?

In general, *tactics that stimulate you work best*. Actors soon learn that verbs like "to tell," "to inform," "to explain," and "to ask" don't make good objectives; frankly, they prove boring on stage. More charged language, however, can provoke specific actions or emotional involvement by the actor. Verbs such as "to challenge," "to inspire," "to encourage," "to probe," or "to justify" help energize performances. There is certainly a time and place for charged and uncharged language in and out of class. Being aware of these dynamics, however, can provide some new breadth to your teaching repertoire, some energizing new choices. For example, in the chapters on development and discovery, we describe approaches that require a very different role from the teacher who is used to lecturing, very different goals and objectives indeed.

Of course, a planned tactic may not work. In any interaction, both parties have tactics that they are using to achieve their objectives. When one tactic meets another that is incompatible, as in the improvised teacher/student conflict, one or both parties must adjust. It is difficult to continue "to charm" if the other person's tactic is "to humiliate." As we've suggested elsewhere in this book, when you are alert to it, you can "read" student reactions, whether verbal or nonverbal, and possibly switch tactics when necessary.

Gibberish

Spolin uses gibberish exercises extensively in her improvisational training program for actors. Speaking in gibberish requires the performer to substitute "shaped sounds for recognizable words." The performer talks in nonsense syllables and, in effect, creates a new language. "Open the door" may become, for instance, "Oo gla-gla!" or "Shripti seeps!" — depending on who gives the command. As Spolin (1983, 120) explains, "Gibberish is a vocal utterance accompanying an action, not the translation of an English phrase. The meaning of a sound in gibberish should not be understood unless the actor conveys it by his action, expressions, or tone of voice."

Working with gibberish enhances the actor's facility with nonverbal expression. As Spolin (1983, 120) points out, "Gibberish develops the expressive physical language vital to stage life, by removing the dependency on words alone to express meaning."

As a teacher seeking to develop your expressive qualities, you too may benefit from gibberish exercises. In essence it's a consciousness-raising activity. Most teachers dominate the talk time available in class. If you lecture, you may see that as your responsibility. However, a key question for you is the following: How much "space" could be opened in class — for reflection, interaction, discussion, and a deeper kind of learning — if you make more use of nonverbal communications? Try the following series of gibberish improvs with your support group.

A word of encouragement may be needed here. As a teacher, you are undoubtedly quite comfortable with speaking in front of groups. Indeed, you may well enjoy the spotlight and the challenge. Undertaking an exercise that takes away your language, your traditional source of communication, can be intimidating. Trust us: getting past these natural anxieties and creating a new language can make you more aware of nonverbal factors that affect communication. Besides, it can be great fun. And, if you can do these exercises, *you can do anything!* Go for it!

Part 1
Start by practicing simple commands in gibberish. Take turns asking someone — in gibberish — to stand up, sit down, open a window, sing a scale, etc. Accompany the command with a gesture. Continue communicating until the person understands the command and performs the desired action.

Part 2
Select two players at random and ask them to go "on stage," with no preparation. Each player in turn uses gibberish to tell the other about something that has happened to him or her, while the rest of the group observes.

Processing
Questions to consider:

- Ask the first player what the second player said.

- Ask the second player what the first player said.

- Ask the others what was communicated to them by each of the players.

- Did the players solve the problem of communicating with gibberish?

Part 3

Ask each player in turn to go "on stage" and sell or demonstrate something to the audience in gibberish. The player is to "pitch" a product to the others, making direct eye contact with them.

Processing
Questions to consider:

- Ask the audience to describe what the performer communicated to them.

- Did the performer make genuine contact with the audience?

- Did the performer solve the problem?

Part 4

Select two teams of two players each. One member of each team plays the "ambassador" and one the "translator." Both members of a team speak the same gibberish language; give them a few minutes to work together to develop their shared "language." (Note: They should not attempt to come up with "definitions" for particular sounds, but rather create a particular kind of sound "language." For instance, one language might be very sibilant or hissing, another very guttural, from back in the throat, etc.)

Then give the teams a particular conflict situation to improvise. For instance, the two ambassadors might be meeting to try to negotiate a peace treaty, solve a border dispute, or reach a trade agreement. Each ambassador will speak to a translator only in their established gibberish language. (The ambassadors supposedly do not understand English.) The translators will speak to each other in English. Each translator must translate the other ambassador's demands (as expressed by that ambassador's translator) into gibberish and then translate into English — as accurately as possible — whatever his or her ambassador replies. After the ambassadors reach an agreement (or declare war!), discuss the exercise.

Processing
Questions to consider:

- Ask each ambassador about the accuracy of the translations.

- Ask each translator how fully his or her ambassador communicated.

- Ask the audience what each player communicated to them. Did the players solve the problem?

When performers first start working with gibberish, they tend to communicate with elaborate, detailed pantomimes, trying to substitute illustrative gestures for the words on which they normally rely. As actors become more "fluent" in gibberish, their responses become more organic — and more subtle.

Gibberish work intensifies the actor's focus on communication and awareness of nuances. The performer must really concentrate on listening, observing, and opening up to others in order to communicate successfully with gibberish. Because this exercise requires intense and direct connection with other people, the person who habitually relies solely on words to communicate often resists.

An excessive reliance on words to communicate, however, can get in the way of genuine communication. Spolin (1983, 121) quotes one student who found gibberish difficult and anxiety-producing: "You are on your own when you speak gibberish! When you use words, people know the words you are saying. So you don't have to do anything yourself." Do we teachers rely too much on our words to do all the work?

Part 5

After the players have become comfortable with gibberish, ask each to present a section of an actual lecture — in gibberish. Again, ask the audience members what the player communicated to them. Then have the player repeat the same section of the lecture in English.

Processing

Questions to consider:

- Ask the audience what they understood from the gibberish lecture. What was different when English was used? Which was more interesting? More energetic?

- In which version did the lecturer concentrate more on communicating?

- Did any of the gestures, intonations, etc., "carry over" from the gibberish to the English version?

Role Wheel

In our chapter on questions, answers, and discussions, we introduced the concept of the role wheel as a "hook" to stimulate class discussion. We suggest that you and your group experiment with role wheels. If you need to, review our description of it. Working in pairs, each person plays one role for two to three minutes and then switches roles. For the next situation, move along the "wheel" and pick another partner.

Situation 1

Character A: Student. You've received your semester grades and find that your grade point average has fallen below the level needed to maintain your scholarship. Losing the scholarship would cause financial hardship for you. You ask the teacher of a course in which you received a C if there's any way you could get the grade raised.

Character B: Teacher. The administration has complained about grade inflation and also about the large number of grade changes professors have been making in recent years. (*Note:* The person playing the teacher should establish the nature of the course.)

Situation 2

Character A: Teacher. A student in one of your introductory courses shows exceptional promise for your field. You talk to the student to encourage him or her to become a major. (*Note:* The person playing the teacher should establish the course and the field.)

Character B: Student. This is your favorite class and you find yourself fascinated by the subject. However, you and your parents have planned for you to pursue a different professional career, one that you consider more lucrative.

Situation 3

Character A: Teacher. You've been teaching for a number of years. When you started, you loved teaching, but now you're feeling burned out and you resent the long hours and low pay. You've been offered a job outside of academia that offers a substantially better salary and you're considering taking it.

Character B: Student. This particular teacher has been your mentor and a wonderful teacher. You hear that he or she has been thinking about giving up teaching and you don't want that to happen, so you approach him or her.

Processing Part 1
Questions to consider:

- In which of the situations were you most engaged? Why?

- Have you had an experience similar to any of those in the role wheel? How did you handle that situation?

- What did you learn from the role reversal? Did everyone handle the situation the same way?

- What issues did the role wheel raise? How do you feel about those issues?

Processing Part 2
After processing the role wheel experience, discuss the role wheel as an exercise.

Questions to consider:

- Were the instructions clear?

- Could the description of the situations be improved? If so, how?

- Did you have enough time in each situation? Too much?

- What was the value of the role reversal? Did the role wheel stimulate significant discussion? How?

- Is this an effective way to surface tough issues and air them among friends and colleagues? How could this kind of exercise help students?

Following the initial experience with the role wheel, we suggest that each member of the group design an activity suitable for use in class. In subsequent meetings, group members can then take turns leading and processing their role wheels. After each "rehearsal," the other members can provide feedback on role wheel design and facilitation before the member in question tries the role wheel in class.

Summary

We certainly hope that you will explore these exercises and the impact that they can have on your teaching. We continue to explore possibilities in our own courses and with colleagues. Let us know what works for you, what doesn't, and what other ideas you might have. We'd love to hear from you!

Scenes for Practice, Fun, and Exploration

Having experienced acting exercises and their application to teaching, we suggest you look at a few plays and movies that deal with teaching. Read the plays for the insights they provide — or, better yet, explore each as a script to act. Put yourself into the characters of the teachers and students these dramatists portray. Use the acting techniques you've been learning as you read a scene aloud with other group members. Watch the movies to see how professionals played these characters.

Have you ever found yourself in situations similar to those depicted in these plays and films? How did you handle them?

Our "top pick" of plays and films:

Plays

Mamet, David. 1992. *Oleanna.* New York: Vintage.

This play has stirred up a good deal of controversy in its portrayal of a male professor caught up in an increasingly explosive series of interactions with a female student. As the play unfolds in the professor's office, his intellectual glibness, ambition, and distractibility clash with the student's struggles to learn and her growing resentment. Power? Helplessness? Ambition? Misunderstandings? Revenge? Victimization? And then — violence!

Some of the controversy revolves around the various ways of playing the characters. When the professor is played as an arrogant academic type obsessed with his own career and impending purchase of a home, you get a more traditional victimization of a younger and less powerful female. However, when the professor is played as a relatively innocent victim of the effort of an unnamed group to confront an "oppressive academic patriarchy," you get a reversal of traditional roles — and more controversy.

In the first scene of the play, Carol (the student) has come to talk to John (her professor) about her answer on an exam, which received a low grade. Try performing a section of this scene — for instance, from the top of page 11 to the end of the first line on page 15. Act the scene from each of the two perspectives described above: first, where the professor is caught up in his role as expert and insensitive to a struggling student; second, where the student intends to entrap the professor in order to further a political agenda. Are there other ways to play this scene?

Wilson, Lanford. 1982. *Angels Fall*. New York: Hill and Wang.

Niles is a college professor of art history experiencing a crisis of faith in his profession, recognizing his failure to educate students to think for themselves rather than to simply accept his word — or anyone else's — as gospel. After rethinking his role as expert, he rips up his books in front of his students and announces an end to irrelevant "brainwashing." His college administration ships him off to a fancy sanitorium; while en route, Niles and his wife Vita are trapped by a disaster at a nuclear plant into taking shelter in a little adobe mission in New Mexico. Try performing the scene on pages 86-90 (beginning with Niles' monologue) in which Niles explores his decision to renounce teaching. Think of the ways in which you could play Niles — a true heretic, slightly crazed, an idealist, a fool, a teacher who could inspire the young. Have you ever felt like Niles? Do you agree or disagree with Father Doherty's belief that teaching is a sacred "calling"?

Russell, Willy. 1981. *Educating Rita*. New York: Samuel French.

This play explores the relationship that develops between Frank, an alcoholic literature professor at a British university, and Rita, a commoner and a hairdresser, as Frank attempts to tutor Rita. In the process, both discover something about what education really means. With a partner, read the scene on pages 18-22 (Act I, Scene 4). What does education mean to Frank? To Rita?

Albee, Edward. 1962. *Who's Afraid of Virginia Woolf?* New York: Pocket Books.

This savage play depicts the stormy relationship between George, a history professor at a small college, and his wife Martha, daughter of the college's president. Although the play has little direct reference to the classroom, it conveys a sense of the seamy side of campus politics. George, a "bookish" type, fails to live up to Martha's plans for him to become an administrator, her father's "heir." Her frustrated ambition drives her to belittle him in front of their guests: Nick, a junior faculty member new to the college, and his "mousy" wife, Honey. Explore, for instance, the scene at the end of Act I (pages 75-86, beginning with Martha's line at the bottom of the page).

Actors develop a full biography for each character they play, embellishing the "given circumstances" in the script with imagined details. Based on the clues given in *Who's Afraid of Virginia Woolf?*, imagine each character's life. How will different choices about the character biography affect the way each role is played and the lines delivered? Do you know a Martha, George, Nick, or Honey on your campus?

Videotapes

Educating Rita (1963)

Julie Walters plays a Cockney hairdresser who entices her professor (Michael Caine) into teaching her about the literary world and, in the process, she lifts him out of his professional doldrums. Witty, touching. Directed by Lewis Gilbert.

Who's Afraid of Virginia Woolf? (1966)

Gripping adaptation of the Broadway hit about a middle-aged professor (Richard Burton) and his wife (Elizabeth Taylor), whose volatile relationship moves from feigned sophistication to abusive, from witty to ugly, in the company of their guests, Nick (George Segal) and Honey (Sandy Dennis). Directed by Mike Nichols.

The Paper Chase (1973)

First-year students at Harvard Law School must face their most feared professor (Oscar-winning John Houseman). His daughter (Lindsay Wagner) and one of his students (Timothy Bottoms) then provide an element of light comic romance as a counterweight to the serious academic pursuits. Directed by James Bridges.

References

Abel, Lionel. 1963. *Metatheatre: A new view of dramatic form*. New York: Hill and Wang.

Andrew, Desley, William Timpson, and Duncan Nulty. 1994. Feedback on and assessment of tertiary instruction. *Tertiary Education News* 4(3):9-16.
A review of the literature on student evaluation of teaching in higher education. In general, there is overwhelming evidence that students are reliable and fair judges of a teacher's effectiveness. This conclusion strengthens our case for being more aware of our students and benefiting from their feedback.

Ausubel, David Paul. 1963. *The psychology of meaningful verbal learning: An introduction to school learning*. New York: Grune and Stratton.
Basic research, with groundbreaking work on the advance organizer, a concept that can help you focus student attention on the underlying conceptual structure of a topic.

Barish, Jonas. 1981. *The antitheatrical prejudice*. Berkeley: University of California Press.

Barton, Robert. 1989. *Acting: Onstage and off*. New York: Holt, Rinehart and Winston.
As Barton points out, "Acting is one of the best ways to learn about being alive" (vii). In this text, full of helpful exercises, Barton explores the relationship between acting and daily life, showing how the actor draws upon his/her personal experience in creating a character — and how the acting process can facilitate personal growth.

————. 1993. *Style for actors*. Mountain View, CA: Mayfield Publishing.
This award-winning book, written in a style that engages the student's imagination, is intended to help student actors enter the world of plays from different historical periods. The methodology outlined here could be adapted by teachers to bring a historical period alive for their students.

Bates, Brian. 1987. *The way of the actor: A path to knowledge and power*. Boston: Shambhala.
For readers who want to probe deeper into the ways in which acting can provide a path for self-development, this book contains quotes from numerous actors, including Meryl Streep, Marlon Brando, Glenda Jackson, Liv Ullmann, and Jack Nicholson.

Belenky, Mary Field, Blythe McVicker Clinchy, Nancy Rule Goldberger, and Jill Mattuck Tarule. 1986. *Women's ways of knowing: The development of self, voice, and mind*. New York: Basic Books.
This book makes a persuasive case for attention to gender issues in learning and a more student-centered approach to teaching.

Benedetti, Robert. 1976. *The actor at work*. Englewood Cliffs, NJ: Prentice-Hall.
Excellent acting textbook with lots of exercises to help you develop vocal and physical expressiveness.

Berman, Paul, and Milbrey Wallin McLaughlin. 1975. *Federal programs supporting educational change, vol. VI: A summary of the findings in review*. Santa Monica, CA: The Rand Corporation.
A classic study of the federal efforts at promoting educational change. A number of principles emerged that have since served as guides for others, e.g., the importance of understanding the local context and involving key personnel at that level and a reaffirmation of the value of high expectations.

Bloom, Benjamin S., ed. 1985. *Developing talent in young people*. New York: Ballantine Books.
A very important treatise on the nature of coaching and mentoring in the development of talent across a range of disciplines and activities, including several with performance aspects; i.e., mathematics, music, and sports. If you want to model your professional development after processes common to the stage and solicit more feedback and coaching (direction) about your teaching, then this book may prove quite useful for explaining the underlying dynamics and for helping you think about your relationships with your students.

Bloom, Benjamin S., and R. Clift. 1984. The Phoenix Agenda: Essential reform in teacher education. *Educational Researcher* 13:5-18.

Bloom, Benjamin S., Max Engelhart, Edward J. Furst, W.H. Hill, and David R. Krathwohl. 1956. *Taxonomy of educational objectives: The classification of educational goals. Handbook I: Cognitive domain.* New York: Longman Green.
This hierarchy for cognitive functioning can be a very useful reference for both planning and teaching. At the lowest level, students are asked to acquire particular knowledge, then move up through intellectually more demanding expectations — understanding, application, analysis, synthesis, and evaluation.

Boal, Augusto. 1979. *Theater of the oppressed.* Translated by Charles A. McBride and Maria-Odilia Leal McBride. New York: Urizen.
In this classic adaptation of the work of Paulo Freire to the theatre, audience members become the subjects ("spect-actors") of the actors' skills. The "production" is no longer about a written script, but is developed instead out of the lived experiences of those in attendance. Actors and audience join in exploring possible solutions.

———. 1992. *Games for actors and non-actors.* New York: Routledge.
Building on the work of Paulo Freire, Boal has developed a form of interactive theatre aimed at empowering the audience and facilitating social change. Boal briefly describes the history of his work in exploring real-life issues through the use of theatre exercises and includes numerous exercises that can be adapted for the classroom.

———. 1995. *Rainbow of desire: The Boal method of theatre and therapy.* New York: Routledge.
A summary of Boal's theatre work as applied to education and therapy. Includes references to earlier work as well as new exercises. Again the focus is on increased awareness, personal empowerment, developing new skills and attitudes, exploring new possibilities through group support and assistance, and gaining new insights through nonverbal representations.

Boyer, Ernest L. 1990. *The professoriate reconsidered.* Princeton, NJ: Carnegie Commission.
This report was commissioned to address the long-standing tensions between research and teaching and offer some new ideas. In his recommendations, which have received much attention worldwide, Boyer calls for an expanded notion of scholarship, to go beyond basic research to recognize contributions across a range of activities. Until the creative work that renews and energizes teaching is rewarded, Boyer insists, undergraduates in large classes in particular will continue to be exploited to support research and graduate studies.

Brecht, Bertolt. 1964. *Brecht on theatre: The development of an aesthetic.* Edited and translated by John Willett. New York: Hill and Wang.

Bruner, Jerome S. 1966. *Toward a theory of instruction.* Cambridge, MA: Harvard University Press.
  Important work by a scholar who did some of the most significant research on student learning, particularly on the processes by which students discover and understand concepts. We see much potential here for applying lessons from the stage, to use drama to help inspire interest and promote active, deep learning.

Burns, Morris, and Porter Woods. 1991. *Teacher as actor.* Dubuque, IA: Kendall-Hunt.
  Two theatre professors draw on their experiences with leading workshops for faculty to describe lessons from the stage that are relevant to postsecondary teaching. An easy read with lots of stories from the theatre and the classroom.

Bybee, Rodger W., and Robert B. Sund. 1982. *Piaget for educators.* 2nd ed. Columbus, OH: Merrill.
  It's difficult to get into Piaget, to sift through translations of very dry, academic, and dense prose. This is an accessible interpretation for teachers at all levels.

Clurman, Harold. 1972. *On directing.* New York: Collier.
  A founding member of the influential Group Theatre in the 1930s, Clurman helped introduce the Stanislavski system of acting to the U.S. This book provides valuable examples of directorial analysis of a script, particularly the use of spines (super-objectives).

Cohen, Robert. 1984. *Acting one.* Palo Alto, CA: Mayfield Publishing.
  Good, basic acting text by a popular acting teacher, with exercises for vocal development and inflection that should be especially useful for teachers.

Cole, David. 1992. *Acting as reading: The place of the reading process in the actor's work.* Ann Arbor: University of Michigan Press.

Davis, Robert B., Carolyn A. Maher, and Nel Noddings. 1990. *Constructivist views on the teaching and learning of mathematics.* Reston, VA: National Council of Teachers of Mathematics.
  There is a growing and rich literature on constructivist approaches to teaching and learning, three of which are featured in our text through discussions about the interrelationships between lessons from the stage and ideas about development, discovery, and creativity. Mathematics education, in particular, is criticized for being irrelevant and abstract. Constructivist notions support more active approaches to promote deeper learning.

Delgado, Ramon. 1986. *Acting with both sides of your brain: Perspectives on the creative process.* New York: Holt, Rinehart and Winston.
Ideas about brain hemisphere functioning applied to the acting process. Includes an interesting section on conscious and unconscious role-playing, with specific examples drawn from college life.

Denham, Carolyn, and Ann Lieberman. 1980. *Time to learn.* Washington, DC: National Institute of Education, Program on Teaching and Learning.
This work summarizes what is known about engaged learning, an important concept when looking at teaching from the perspective of the stage. Beginning with the time allotted and then subtracting time lost to tardiness or announcements and the like, teachers have a subset of time defined as "instructional." Subtracting time when students are off task produces another subset labeled here as "engaged time." Subtracting time when students are *not* learning produces a final inner subset, when they are indeed successful. An even smaller subset could include time when students are challenged to go from surface to deep learning. Much described in our text about the various lessons from the stage point toward these two inner subsets.

Dickens, Charles. 1854. *Hard times.* Edited by Grahame Smith, London: Everyman.
Some classic scenes from an earlier era of schooling when the mastery of facts meant everything. Fun to portray. Potentially provocative as a stimulus for discussion: representing an extreme position can allow for more open and frank exchange of opinions and beliefs.

Dreikurs, Rudolf. 1968. *Psychology in the classroom: A manual for teachers.* New York: Harper & Row.
Teachers can benefit greatly from understanding student motivations and learning how to channel potentially disruptive intentions into constructive directions that support learning.

Eble, Kenneth E. 1994. *The craft of teaching.* 3rd ed. San Francisco: Jossey-Bass.
One of the most cited books on teaching in higher education. Readable, with lots of good ideas and solid recommendations.

Erikson, Erik H. 1974. *Dimensions of a new identity.* New York: Norton.
No discussion of development could be complete without some mention of Erikson and the crises that we all confront as we move through life. For teachers in higher education, advanced stages have special relevance, as wisdom and skills are passed on to the next generation.

Freire, Paulo. 1970. *Pedagogy of the oppressed.* New York: Seabury.

A classic work that describes a paradigm, a philosophy, and practices that promote student empowerment. Freire extols active and cooperative learning, building blocks for many of the principles and techniques in the performing arts.

Fullan, Michael, with Suzanne Stiegelbauer. 1991. *The new meaning of educational change.* New York: Teachers College Press, Columbia University.
The most referenced review of the literature on educational change. Although the focus is primarily on elementary and secondary schools, most of the conclusions seem to hold for higher education. Although most relevant from the perspective of systems, there are lots of findings that can help you plan for professional development, i.e., the importance of feedback, local models, support, and assistance.

Gilligan, Carol. 1982. *In a different voice: Psychological theory and women's development.* Cambridge, MA: Harvard University Press.
A very important critique of the dominant Kohlberg model of moral development, offering an alternative view of women. Considerations of gender and diversity in learning become especially important in a developmental perspective of education, with its emphasis on stimulating and challenging students, on involving them more actively, and on showing greater sensitivity to individual needs.

Glasser, William. 1965. *Reality therapy: A new approach to psychiatry.* New York: Harper & Row.

————. 1969. *Schools without failure.* New York: Harper & Row.
Although his focus is on elementary and secondary school teaching, Glasser argues for the centrality of student self-worth and the use of non-judgmental acceptance by teachers. As we explore new roles and stretch to develop new skills, as performers and as teachers, it becomes more important to have a professional climate that is also supportive and non-judgmental.

Gleick, James. 1987. *Chaos: Making a new science.* New York: Viking Penguin.
A difficult but important description of the origins of chaos theory. Even if you can't follow all the math, the story reaffirms the place for what is non-linear, unpredictable. It's truly humbling what we don't know. Should humility have a bigger role in our classes?

Goffman, Erving. 1959. *The presentation of self in everyday life.* New York: Doubleday Anchor.

Gordon, William J.J. 1961. *Synectics: The development of creative capacity.* New York: Harper.

Groundbreaking work that has helped to demystify the nature and development of creativity.

Grant, Barbara M., and Dorothy Grant Hennings. 1971. *The teacher moves: An analysis of nonverbal activity.* New York: Teachers College Press, Columbia University.
Important analysis of the interrelationships between teaching and moving — the potential of gestures and movements generally, either to distract students or to help them learn.

Grotowski, Jerzy. 1968. *Towards a poor theatre.* New York: Simon and Schuster.

Hagen, Uta, with Haskel Frankel. 1973. *Respect for acting.* New York: Macmillan.
A first-person description of the acting process by a major American actress/teacher.

Hornby, Richard. 1986. *Drama, metadrama, and perception.* Lewisburg, PA: Bucknell University Press.

Hunter, Madeline. 1982. *Mastery teaching.* El Segundo, CA: TIP Publications.
Written for teachers at all levels as a concise summary of relevant research on effective teaching, this book has proven particularly popular among elementary and secondary teachers. The concepts described here can serve as a common language for teachers from different disciplines to discuss common problems, share ideas, and collaborate on improvement activities. You will find much support here for recommendations from the stage, particularly using multimodal approaches and "teaching to both sides of the brain."

Johnson, David W., and Roger T. Johnson. 1994. *Learning together and alone: Cooperative, collaborative, and individualistic learning.* Needham Heights, MA: Allyn and Bacon.
Summarizing years of research and numerous studies, the Johnson brothers make a very strong case for cooperative learning. Bubbling with the confidence of near-zealots, they attack competitive and individualized learning as anachronistic, ineffective, and divorced from the real world. Although writing primarily for elementary and secondary teachers, they present many practical ideas that are quite relevant for higher education.

Johnson, David W., Roger T. Johnson, and Karl Smith. 1989. *Cooperative learning: Cooperation and competition, theory and research.* Edina, MN: Interaction Book Co.
Excellent, full of references on the value and use of cooperative learning in higher education.

Johnstone, Keith. 1979. *IMPRO: Improvisation and the theatre*. New York: Theatre Arts Books.
A pioneer in British educational theatre, Johnstone explores the use of improvisational exercises to free the creative imagination from what he sees as the numbing effects of social conditioning. He recounts: "As I grew up, everything started getting gray and dull. I could still remember the amazing intensity of the world I'd lived in as a child, but I thought the dulling of perception was an inevitable consequence of age. ... I've since found tricks that can make the world blaze up again in about fifteen seconds, and the effects last for hours. ... In a normal education everything is designed to suppress spontaneity, but I wanted to develop it" (13, 15).

Joyce, Bruce R., and Beverly Showers. 1978. The coaching of teaching. *Educational Leadership* 40:4-10.
Critiquing the professional isolation that encases teaching at every level, Joyce and Showers categorize the different kinds of coaching that can improve teaching and describe processes that mirror what performers undergo during the rehearsal process.

Kohlberg, Lawrence. 1981. *The philosophy of moral development: Moral stages and the idea of justice*. New York: Harper & Row.
Although controversial in its presumed hierarchy and generalizability, this book continues to prove valuable for many teachers. In his call for dilemmas as catalysts for classroom discussions, Kohlberg makes a strong case for using the dramatic to engage the minds and feelings of students and thereby promote higher levels of moral judgment.

Kounin, Jacob S. 1970. *Discipline and group management in classrooms*. New York: Holt, Rinehart and Winston.
The first use of the term "with it" to describe those teachers who were ever aware of what was happening in their classes — which students were struggling, who was disengaged, when a change was needed. An important concept for the discussion of spontaneity, creativity, and "audience awareness" in teaching.

Kuhn, Thomas S. 1970. *The structure of scientific revolutions*. 2nd ed. Chicago: University of Chicago Press.
The classic description of the paradigm shifts that occur in every discipline when new ideas change the way people think. For us, promoting the value of the performing paradigm for education often has the feel of heresy.

Lessinger, Leon M., and Don Gillis. 1976. *Teaching as a performing art*. Edited by Judy Bates. Dallas: Crescendo Publications.

Levinson, Daniel J. 1978. *The seasons of a man's life*. New York: Ballantine Books.

Levinson, Daniel J., with Judy D. Levinson. 1996. *The seasons of a woman's life*. New York: Knopf.
This book, and the previous entry, describe the stages and markers for adult development. Actors must study their characters to understand underlying motivations and — more important — they must know themselves, how best to draw on their strengths and overcome their weaknesses. Unfortunately, teachers often neglect formal attention to their own developmental needs. Through coaching, for example, experienced teachers and performers can offer much of value to new recruits. And through lifelong learning, both teachers and performers can stay alert to the world, to what can be used in the classroom and on stage.

Lortie, Dan C. 1975. *Schoolteacher: A sociological study*. Chicago: University of Chicago Press.

Lowman, Joseph. 1995. *Mastering the techniques of teaching*. 2nd ed. San Francisco: Jossey-Bass.
In one of the best books on teaching in higher education, Lowman provides much practical advice, along with a conclusion that stresses two primary factors in effective teaching — intellectual excitement and interpersonal rapport. Great teaching requires much more than expertise and the transmission of knowledge. The link to the stage is obvious and compelling.

Marsh, Herbert W. 1987. Students' evaluations of university teaching: Research findings, methodological issues, and directions for future research. *International Journal of Educational Research* 11:253-388.
Summary of the existing research, with much evidence for the essential reliability and validity of student evaluations of teaching.

Maslow, Abraham H. 1954. *Motivation and personality*. New York: Harper and Brothers.
Maslow remains a seminal figure in the area of human motivation. Whether you focus on your needs as a teacher or those of your students, you may find it useful to understand more about the hierarchy of needs, from survival up to self-actualization. At the highest levels you may find more value in lessons from the stage, as you try to develop more creative and engaging approaches to promote deeper learning.

McGaw, Charles, and Larry D. Clark. 1992. *Acting is believing: A basic method*. 6th ed. Fort Worth, TX: Harcourt Brace Jovanovich.
We find this a very useful text for teachers, as it ascribes much success on stage to an actor's ability to really understand a character at a deep level. At another level, we like this text because of what it implies about the teacher's role, how care about the subject combines with a core belief in student abilities, to energize instruction and empower learning.

McKeachie, Wilbert J. 1994. *Teaching tips: A guidebook for the beginning college teacher.* 9th ed. Lexington, MA: D.C. Heath.
A classic, with very little theory and lots of specific ideas and suggestions — the nuts and bolts of teaching in higher education.

McLaren, Peter. 1988. The liminal servant and the ritual roots of critical pedagogy. *Language Arts* 65:164-179.

McLaughlin, Milbrey W. 1990. The Rand Change Agent Study revisited: Macro perspectives and micro realities. *Educational Researcher* 19:11-16.
McLaughlin reaffirms the power of credible, local role models as catalysts for changing teacher behaviors and attitudes. The peer feedback/coaching model that we recommend uses teaching colleagues and classroom observations and closely parallels the rehearsal/direction process essential for stage productions.

McLaughlin, Milbrey W., R. Scott Pfeifer, Deborah Seanson-Ownes, and Sylvia Yee. 1986. Why teachers won't teach. *Phi Delta Kappan* 67:420-426.

Miller, Arthur. 1967. The American theatre. In *Death of a Salesman: Text and criticism*, edited by Gerald Weales. New York: Viking Press.

Moore, Sonia. 1984. *The Stanislavski System: The professional training of an actor.* 2nd ed. New York: Penguin.
A concise introduction to the acting principles developed by Konstantin Stanislavski, the founder of modern acting theory and practice.

Perry, William J., Jr. 1981. Cognitive and ethical growth: The making of meaning. In *The modern American college: Responding to the new realities of diverse students and a changing society,* edited by Arthur W. Chickering and Associates. San Francisco: Jossey-Bass.
In what may be the most frequently cited reference about the cognitive development of college students, Perry describes the shifts that allow the 22-year-old to understand a greater diversity of opinion and handle increasing levels of complexity. Here again, teachers can benefit from the stage, as great theatre can offer a range of characters and conflicts, multiple levels of meaning, and intellectual stimulation.

Peters, Thomas J., and Nancy Austin. 1985. *A passion for excellence: The leadership difference.* New York: Random House.
The authors sift the evidence down to two qualities that seem to drive successful companies — caring for the customer and innovation. We find it most interesting that these two qualities also drive stage performances, but are too often neglected in postsecondary teaching, where the focus is too often on "covering the material."

Peters, Thomas J., and Robert H. Waterman, Jr. 1982. *In search of excellence: Lessons from America's best-run companies.* New York: Harper & Row.
We are impressed by the conclusions here, which match many of our arguments about relevant lessons from the stage — such as "staying close to the knitting" (student learning/audience engagement) and "management by walking around" (close monitoring of student reactions/direction and feedback through rehearsal).

Piaget, Jean. 1952. *The origins of intelligence in children.* New York: International Universities Press.
Although most of his research focused on children, Piaget identified several principles and concepts that are relevant for college students and our arguments for the theatre analogy. Often overlooked are those factors that impact the learning of the very young and that continue to play a role throughout life. These findings suggest that active and experiential learning can be important at every level of education.
Note: Bybee and Sund (1982) have provided a good interpretation of Piaget for teachers at all levels.

Pineau, Elyse Lamm. 1994. Teaching is performance: Reconceptualizing a problematic metaphor. *American Educational Research Journal* 31(1):3-25.

Polsky, Milton E. 1980. *Let's improvise: Becoming creative, expressive and spontaneous through drama.* Englewood Cliffs, NJ: Prentice-Hall.
A highly accessible introduction to unleashing creativity through dramatic improvisation. Polsky includes a chapter on using role-play as a teaching tool in the classroom.

Postlewait, Thomas, and Bruce A. McConachie, eds. 1989. *Interpreting the theatrical past: Essays in the historiography of performance.* Iowa City: University of Iowa Press.

Ramsden, Paul. 1992. *Learning to teach in higher education.* London: Routledge.
An especially popular book in the United Kingdom and Australia. Ramsden makes a simple and direct appeal to shift the focus from teaching to the needs of the learner.

Rogers, Carl R. 1951. *Client-centered therapy: Its current practices, implications, and theory.* Boston: Houghton Mifflin.
A classic relevant to any student-centered focus for instruction. Rogers emphasizes acceptance, listening, and empathy, which can prove particularly valuable in terms of the experiential and developmental emphasis of many of the lessons from the stage described here.

Rogoff, Barbara. 1990. *Apprenticeship in thinking: Cognitive development in social context.* New York: Oxford University Press.
A good argument for "conversations" about "teaching" when the focus is deep learning (i.e., understanding what is constructed and made meaningful).

Sarason, Seymour Bernard. 1984. *The nature of schools and the problem of change.* Boston: Allyn and Bacon.
Often cited in the literature on educational change, Sarason is a clinical psychologist who has catalogued the stress that isolation causes for teachers in the classroom. In the theatre, members of a production build a sense of community through working together. Using peer feedback and coaching can help teachers do the same.

Schechner, Richard. 1985. *Between theatre and anthropology.* Philadelphia: University of Pennsylvania Press.

Schon, Donald A. 1983. *The reflective practitioner: How professionals think in action.* New York: Basic Books.

Seldin, Peter. 1993. *The teaching portfolio: A practical guide to improved performance and promotion/tenure decisions.* Bolton, MA: Anker Publishing.
A practical and concise volume that describes the advantages and possible components of portfolios for teaching.

Shurtleff, Michael. 1978. *Audition: Everything an actor needs to know to get the part.* New York: Walker and Co.

Smiley, Sam. 1971. *Playwriting: The structure of action.* Englewood Cliffs, NJ: Prentice-Hall.
If you want to explore the possibility of structuring your lectures like plays, then this text by a master playwright and teacher can give you insight into how playwrights do it.

Smith, Ralph. 1979. Is teaching really a performing art? *Contemporary Education* 51:31-35.

Spolin, Viola. 1983. *Improvisation for the theater.* Evanston, IL: Northwestern University Press.
Excellent guide to exploring spontaneity, with lots of good exercises that are both fun and revealing. Often quoted by performers, this book is quite accessible to teachers.

———. 1985. *Theater games for rehearsal: A director's handbook.* Evanston, IL: Northwestern University Press.
More exercises and improvisations from the "mother" of American improvisational theatre.

Shurtleff, Michael. 1978. *Audition: Everything an actor needs to know to get the part.* New York: Walker and Co.

Swanson, Charles H. 1980. Our medium is our message: Potentials for educational theatre. *Theatre Quarterly* 9:61-65.

Tauber, Robert T., and Cathy Sargent Mester. 1994. *Acting lessons for teachers: Using performance skills in the classroom.* Westport, CT: Praeger Publishers.

Tharp, Roland, and Ronald Gallimore. 1988. *Rousing minds to life: Teaching, learning, and schooling in social context.* Cambridge, UK; New York: Cambridge University Press.
An acclaimed new argument for instruction that is active and engaging, emphasizing the importance of "conversations" with students and the learning that they construct out of their involvement in their communities.

Timpson, William M. 1988. Paulo Freire: Advocate of literacy through liberation. *Educational Leadership* 45:62-66.
Nicaragua, Cuba, and Brazil inspired dramatic increases in literacy by turning traditional teaching on its head, using small study groups and materials that built upon the skills, experiences, and hopes of students.

Timpson, William M., and Paul Bendel-Simso. 1996. *Concepts and choices for teaching: Meeting the challenges in higher education.* Madison, WI: Magna Publications.
This book reviews the most important research on teaching and learning and describes the concepts that underlie effective instruction. The range of choices can produce very different results and allow teachers to organize instruction in various ways.

Timpson, William M., and David N. Tobin. 1982. *Teaching as performing: A guide to energizing your public presentation.* Englewood Cliffs, NJ: Prentice-Hall.
Treated as somewhat heretical by scholars who have focused on the "science" of teaching, this short and practical book seemed to threaten teachers who wanted to stay focused on content and feared any discussion of the parallels between the classroom and the stage.

Tobias, Sheila. 1990. *They're not dumb, they're different.* Tucson, AZ: Research Corporation.
Tobias interviewed students who quit as science majors, then succeeded in other disciplines. Her resulting indictment of the ways in which large introductory science classes are typically taught has proven quite telling. In particular, large numbers of female and minority students reported feeling discouraged when classes were impersonal, competitive, and judgmental. Here again, we see benefits from the stage, where the cast and

crew tackle a production as an ensemble. Traditional instruction can incorporate more cooperative learning, with its emphasis on peer support and assistance.

Tobin, Kenneth. 1983. The influence of wait-time on classroom learning. *European Journal of Science Education* 5:35-48.
Teachers can overcome some problems with participation by waiting more patiently for students to respond to questions.

Toffler, Alvin, ed. 1974. *Learning for tomorrow: The role of the future in education.* New York: Random House.

Turner, Victor. 1982. *From ritual to theatre: The human seriousness of play.* New York: Performing Arts Journal Publications.

von Oech, Roger. 1983. *A whack on the side of the head: How to unlock your mind for innovation.* New York: Warner Books.
Fun and accessible, for you and your students. Once you accept the importance of creativity in teaching, a whole world can open up. From mind locks to myths, a quick skip through the terrain, with lots of activities to try.

————. 1986. *A kick in the seat of the pants: Using your explorer, artist, judge, and warrior to be more creative.* New York: Warner Books.
The *explorer* in us investigates new possibilities. Our *artist* persona can see aesthetic values. Our *judge* has to make some decisions. Then our *warrior* puts these decisions into action. A fun, light, and easy read with some lasting value — for you and your students.

Wilsey, C., and J. Killion. 1982. Making staff development programs work. *Educational Leadership* 40:36-43.

Wilshire, Bruce. 1982. *Role playing and identity: The limits of theatre as metaphor.* Bloomington: Indiana University Press.

Wirth, Jeff. 1994. *Interactive acting: Acting, improvisation, and interacting for audience participatory theatre.* Fall Creek, OR: Fall Creek Press.
Drawing on the work of Augusto Boal, Playback Theatre, and other forms of improvisatory theatre that elicit audience participation, Wirth offers s pecific suggestions for actors and directors, many of which are relevant for teachers wishing to use role-playing exercises in their classrooms.

Yager, Robert E. 1991. The constructivist learning model. *The Science Teacher* 58(6) (September):53-57.
Much work in science education is now pointing toward more attention to active, hands-on, and engaged learning as a foundation for shifting from a surface learning of terminology and facts toward a deeper understanding

of more abstract and theoretical constructs. (See Davis et al., 1990, cited above.)

Young, T.R. 1990. *The drama of social life: Essays in post-modern social psychology*. New Brunswick, NJ: Transaction Publishers.

Zukav, Gary. 1984. *The dancing Wu Li masters: An overview of the new physics*. London: Fontana.
A wonderful read about research in physics and the ways in which Eastern ideas about intuition and wonder can be vital companions to a more reductionist approach to science and discovery. Drawing an analogy from the arts, Zukav describes the best teaching as a dance where learners are led through the material in an intimate series of turns and steps.

Index